THE AUTHORITY MINDSET

Proven Principles For Establishing Yourself
as an Expert in Any Industry

Authors

David Bame, Jr.
Nora Benyahya
John P. Berry
Dustin Briley
Tim Chermak
Noble Crawford III
Roger Due
Valerie DuVall
Eloise Edwards-Giron
T. Allen Hanes
Elizabeth Hartenberger
Brian Horn

Art Koster
Victor Little
Kurt Lucien
Stephanie Miller
Jack Mize
James Moux, MBA
Diana M. Needham
Brian Richards
Glen Rothquel
Ken Sherman
Louis F. Vargas

Copyright © 2014 Authority Media Group, LLC

Published by Authority Media Group, LLC Houston, TX

ISBN: 978-1500825454

The Publisher has strived to be as accurate and complete as possible in the creation of this book.

This book is not intended for use as a source of legal, business, accounting or financial advice. All readers are advised to seek services of competent professionals in legal, business, accounting, and financial fields.

In practical advice books, like anything else in life, there are no guarantees of income made. Readers are cautioned to rely on their own judgment about their individual circumstances and to act accordingly.

While all attempts have been made to verify information provided in this publication, the Publisher assumes no responsibility for errors, omissions, or contrary interpretation of the subject matter herein. Any perceived slights of specific persons, peoples, or organizations are unintentional.

TABLE OF CONTENTS

INTRODUCTION

You are living in one of the most exciting times for Entrepreneurs and Professionals to take advantage of the huge opportunities available to access the same Secret Strategies used by national business gurus to establish INSTANT CREDIBILITY AND TRUST!

So why are so many business owners, speakers, coaches, and consultants struggling to gain attention while others, perhaps even less qualified or deserving, are being recognized as the expert... the AUTHORITY in their industry?

It's not necessarily because they are better or smarter at their craft. In fact, that's rarely the case. The truth is, they are doing the right things that make it easy for others to call them the expert. More importantly, they are not waiting for someone else to come and "anoint" them as the authority. They are taking control and architecting their ascent with purpose and a plan.

Authority Positioning

There are a lot more ways to do it wrong than there are to do it right. Most business owners are doing it wrong, or completely neglecting it all together. Before you ever make a decision on a website, a video, social media, book, or any kind of content, for that matter, you need to know how you are going to apply these to your business to get the most effective authority positioning.

You need to understand what your message should be, who your message is for, and why your message will inspire authority regardless of what medium you use to deliver it.

A successful message positions you as an authority, inspiring prospects to pick you, and make your current clients want to come back more often – to spend more money, and tell their friends, family and even strangers about how great you are.

If your message is unsuccessful, then it doesn't really matter how many websites, videos or books you put your time and effort into.

Before you spend another dollar on traffic to get on the front page of Google, take the time to understand how to get prospects to "pick you," how to turn prospects into clients, and turn those clients into fans by positioning yourself as the Authority in your industry. Like a skilled architect, they are drafting their authority with a purposely designed plan.

What to Expect

We are not going to be talking about any technical stuff for marketing your business. We will be taking a step back and developing the mindset that you must have to quickly and effectively create authority. Then you can use that authority to amplify any and all of your marketing and go far beyond what your competitors are doing or even know exists.

Take a minute to pause and understand why you should be seen as an Authority. What is your direction? Many people just start marketing and they do not really have a clear path. They want to record a video and they hit 'record.' They want to put up a website and they put up a website or Facebook page without any clear direction or purpose to their message.

Purpose and principles are absolutely necessary to make it

effective.

After going through The Authority Mindset you will be crystal clear on that purpose and understand how to apply the principles that will allow others to see you as the Authority.

Behind THE AUTHORITY MINDSET

This book was compiled from conversations, mastermind sessions and the experience of top marketing consultants around the world on the specific and powerful topic of Authority Positioning.

Each contributing author has spent years helping entrepreneurs, business owners and professionals, not just with marketing tactics, but with developing "The Authority Mindset" that is required to gain the expert recognition from prospects, customers and even national media.

You can learn more about each author and what led them to do what they do so well for their clients in the *Profiles of Authority* section of this book.

WHAT IS AUTHORITY POSITIONING?

"When you're small, you need to appear big"

General Sun Tzu – The Art of War

In *The Art of War*, the famous General Sun Tzu said, "When you're small, you need to appear big." Although he probably didn't mean for this simple statement to be marketing advice, it is, indeed, an incredibly important point to remember as entrepreneurs when positioning yourself as an authority in your industry.

So what exactly is an authority when it comes to business? To some it is synonymous with being the expert, thought leader, perhaps even guru of an industry.

Many think expert or authority status can only be attained by convincing enough people that they are smarter than anyone else in their field.

Well, they would be wrong. In fact, what most people consider to be the path to expert status and authority positioning is just unrealistic and as difficult as hunting a unicorn.

So let's be very clear and start with what Authority is NOT.

We want to bust the top five myths that so many entrepreneurs believe are what it takes to be a recognized authority.

Myth #1 — To be an expert, you just need to call yourself an expert.

This has been a popular thought for many, many years in the marketing world. Frankly, it is nothing more than an easy answer to a complex question that is consistently taught to sales people and entrepreneurs. While it may have been mildly effective in the past, it is not how you see most industry leaders achieve their success and reach real authority status.

It goes far beyond that. You can no longer just call yourself an expert and expect the masses to take you at your word. However, you can easily be the person that takes the actions that will make it easy for others to call you the expert.

That is what real authority is: having others recognize you as the expert — and it is simpler than most make it out to be.

Myth #2 — An expert is a person that knows everything about their industry and subject matter.

Well, the fact is that such a person just does not exist. No one knows everything there is about his or her industry, and those that claim they do actually diminish their credibility because people know it is just not possible.

An expert is someone that knows enough to be able to help their customers and their prospects, and they also have to be willing to share that knowledge.

Myth #3 — An expert is the very best at what they do in their field.

You can probably think of someone right now who is considered an expert or an authority in your industry, whether it's fitness, marketing, financial, or real estate. Go ahead; get that person in your mind. Now ask yourself, "Does this person really know any more than I do? Are they the best at what they do?"

So why are they considered the authority? More importantly, *why aren't you?*

Myth # 4 — It takes years to build an expert reputation so that credible media will recognize you as an authority.

Well, that is the slow road that most people take, if they take the road to authority status at all. This is really just an excuse, a logical explanation that we can lean on as to why expert status has not landed on us yet.

Most people think that in order to be considered an expert, they have to work years to build up their reputation by gaining more knowledge, doing that one more thing that will allow them to convince others that they are an expert at what they do. Then maybe, just maybe, someone will come along and recognize them as an expert and then the media will even start to talk about them.

It's a nice story they tell themselves. I'm sure it helps them feel that expert and authority status is coming. It's just down the road.

"Down the road"... that is a dangerous thing to wait for. Especially since the reality is that you can position yourself in the media as an expert *right now*. You can let others see you as an authority because third party credible sources are already talking about you as that expert.

Myth #5 – I'm not ready to step up as an authority right now.

One of the big obstacles that we see hard working entrepreneurs unnecessarily put in front of themselves is the questioning of their own authority.

"Am I really an authority? Am I really an expert? I don't know everything about everything in my industry. I'm just not comfortable calling myself an expert yet... but definitely DOWN THE ROAD."

Write this down, burn it into your brain:

IT IS NOT ABOUT CALLING YOURSELF AN EXPERT!

Let's get this out of the way right now. Commit to yourself that you will never call yourself an expert again.

You also need to commit to yourself that you will freely allow others to call you the expert. Starting right now.

Answer these questions. Don't hesitate or do them later. Do not read another word until you answer these two simple questions.

(1) Do you generally know more than your prospects about your industry, your product, or your service?

(2) Are you willing and able to help your prospects?

If you answered yes to these two questions, then to us, and many of your prospects, you are an EXPERT.

WHAT MAKES ME AN AUTHORITY?

We just told you why you are an authority: You know more than your prospects and clients, and you are willing and able to help them.

Think that's too simple? Let's examine some of the most popular business celebrities from different industries and figure out why they are perceived to be authorities in their field.

Look at people like Dave Ramsey, Suze Orman, Doctor Oz, or Gary Vaynerchuk, and think about their authority positioning in their particular field. Are they the smartest in their fields? Are they the best at what they do in their field? Do they know everything about everything in their industry?

And now that you think about it, do they actually ever call themselves an expert? Do they refer to themselves as THE Authority?

How often do you see them yelling: "Buy my stuff! Buy my stuff!"? Rarely, if ever, right?

So why are they perceived as authorities, even though they are not doing any of the things that so many would have you think you need to do to be considered the expert?

They are not the smartest and they are not the best. They do not call themselves the expert and they are not constantly yelling for you to buy their stuff.

Why? Perhaps it's because they happen to know more than their prospects and customers and they are willing and able to help them.

Wait a minute. What just happened? You want more? We have two words for you.

RICHARD SIMMONS

Yes, Richard "Sweatin' To The Oldies" Simmons. He is a prime example that just demolishes these myths. Think about it.

Why do millions of people buy fitness advice from Richard Simmons?

Now, this is not meant to be derogatory towards Richard Simmons. Quite the opposite, in fact. He is actually the personification of how we define authority. Hold on, stick with us and you will see what we mean.

If you ever feel the need to call yourself an expert, to think you have to be the best at what you do, or think you need to be better than your perceived competitors, just think about Richard Simmons. Is he the healthiest looking person? Is he more fit or more knowledgeable than other fitness gurus? This may not even be debatable.

But what is definitely not debatable is the fact that Richard Simmons has built an empire by knowing more than his prospects and customers about getting healthier, and without a doubt he is willing and able to help those that need it.

So ask yourself again: Richard Simmons, Suze Orman, Doctor Oz, Dave Ramsey – if they are not the best, if they are not the smartest and if they do not know everything about everything about their field, then why are they the authorities? Why are they the expert celebrities in their fields?

There really is a simple answer.

It is because they are **Educators and Advocates** for the success of their prospects and customers.

Read that once more. It is probably the most important point in this book and the reason that you will be recognized as an authority sooner rather than later.

Starting right now, go ahead and remove any fears, worries or pressure that you may have put on yourself to call yourself an expert or to convince others that you're the expert. Simply replace "I'm an expert" with *"I'm an educator and an advocate for the success of my customers and my prospects."*

Do that and you will see something remarkable happen. You will immediately find yourself in the same position as the celebrity authorities in your field.

When you put yourself in the frame of mind of being the educator and the advocate for the success of your prospects and customers, then you will find that you never have to call yourself an expert again.

Others will call you the expert.

Here are some other unfair realities when it comes to authority: When it comes to attracting new customers, it really does not matter if you have a college degree. It does not matter how many products you have purchased. It does not matter how many events you have attended. It does not even matter how hard you work or how good you really are.

An AP-GfK poll suggests only one third of Americans say that most people can be trusted. And if your prospects do not trust or believe you, if they are not convinced that you are an authority, you will have to work ten times as hard to convert them into a customer.

However, if your prospects do trust that you are an authority, if they see others looking at you as an authority, if they see you being an educator and an advocate for their success, then they will pick you over your competition, even if it costs them more to work with you.

Perception is reality. Like it or not, our society has been conditioned to see the media as a credible source of information. They place their trust in the media. They are influenced by recommendations in the media. They give authority to those that are endorsed and seen in the media.

Reader's Digest recently said that the four most trusted people in the world were Tom Hanks, Sandra Bullock, Denzel Washington and Meryl Streep. Well, they are no smarter than you are, no better than you are. In fact, you are probably brilliant compared to ninety-nine percent of the so-called experts featured in the media.

So that is really the simple formula. Getting media sources and third party people talking about you as an educator and advocate can create instant authority for you and your business.

The Chicken or The Egg

Remember the story about the chicken and the egg? Which came first? Do you want to wait and hope that media and third party credible sources might talk about you some day because you spent years calling yourself the expert?

Or would you rather have others see you as the expert right now because credible third party sources are talking about you today?

Well, it is possible. And it is actually easier and more accessible than you think. Becoming an authority and applying the secrets that the business gurus have been using to their advantage for years is something that you can do. But before you think about it, you really have to put yourself in that authority position.

And it is not about convincing your prospects or your clients that you are the expert. It is about convincing yourself that you are an authority.

It simply comes down to this. Can you look your prospects and customers in the eyes and say, "I can help you"?

Once you do that, you will truly become an authority and you can get paid like an authority.

"The simple truth is if you aren't deliberately, systematically, methodically or rapidly and dramatically establishing yourself as a celebrity, at least to your clientele and target market, you're asleep at the wheel, ignoring what is fueling the entire economy around you, neglecting development of a measureable valuable asset."

Dan Kennedy

THE AUTHORITY MINDSET

Let's dig into what it means to be the Educator and Advocate for the success of your prospects and clients.

When a prospect feels that you understand them, sees that you are providing valuable information, and knows that you truly care about their results, they will see you as the expert... as their authority.

One of the misconceptions many entrepreneurs have that prevents them from moving towards authority status is that, as a service provider, they put themselves in a servant position. They feel they need to offer anything and everything to serve their customer.

This takes them out of the role of the authority. When you attempt to serve a prospect by saying, "What would you like? What can I do? I can do anything for you. Tell me what you need me to do and I'll do it," you have shifted from being an authority to being an order taker.

It is the difference between someone that is a landscape architect and someone that simply mows your grass and edges your lawn. The person that mows your grass and edges your lawn is someone you give orders to and tell them what to do. "I want my grass mowed, the hedges trimmed, and the edges cleaned."

However, with the landscape architect you would go to him and say, "What would you suggest? This is what I'm thinking, but what can you do for my yard, for my landscaping?" Your interaction is different because you see that person as an authority.

Be The Doctor

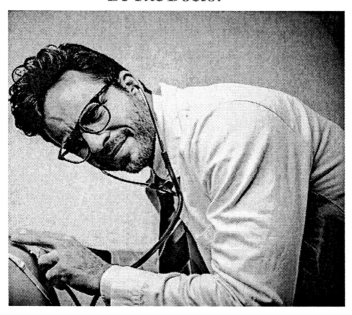

Take a doctor for example. The doctor is someone that you see as an authority. You see them as an expert. Think about when you go to the doctor. You don't get a menu of "Here's what I can do. I can pull out your tonsils. I can give you a shot. I can hit your knee with this hammer. Whatever you want me to do... I can do it."

What would you think? You'd be very concerned and your trust and confidence in that doctor would be very, very low.

You do not go to the doctor to give him or her instructions on what to do for you. You go to get their expert opinion, their advice on a solution to your problem.

That is the position you need to take.

Think about the process. The doctor listens, then the doctor diagnoses, and then the doctor prescribes. That is what an educator and advocate does. The doctor does not say, "I think you should hire me to do this to you. I think you should pay me to do this. Here is my menu. I think you should order this."

What the doctor does is say, "Well, based on what you have told me, my suggestion would be that you do X, Y and Z." When you take that position, you are no longer the salesperson or the servant. You have told them that you listened to them, and based on their situation, offered a solution to their problem. You have just framed yourself as an educator and an advocate for their success.

You still have not asked them to do business with you, but you have made them want to do business with you. You are now apples and oranges compared to anyone else. You have educated them. You are the advocate for their success. You have shown genuine concern for their outcome.

Now, even though you have not asked them to do business, what naturally occurs more often than not is they respond with, "Is that something you can do? Is that something I can hire you to do for me?"

That's when you become the authority. When people try to hide or withhold information from their prospects, in fear that the prospect might want to do it themselves or not hire them, they are doing nothing more than diluting their authority positioning.

An authority is someone that will share. An authority is someone that will educate. An authority will be someone that will not withhold that information. When someone sees you as an authority, they always feel that you have more information than you are sharing. They always feel that what you provide is not a commodity. More importantly, it's not your prices, your tools, or your specific tactics that make them want to work with you.

They chose you because they want to work with *you*. You have shown them to be their educator and advocate. And you are now the authority that they want to hire as their advisor.

So what is the difference between positioning yourself as an expert and positioning yourself as the educator and advocate?

We often find that when someone is ready to be an authority, they feel that they have to do everything possible to convince others they are the expert. How can I make them think I'm the expert without calling myself an expert? What happens is they start making all their content about themselves rather than their prospects. They sound like a walking, talking resume.

We talked earlier that the real power of positioning yourself as an authority is not convincing people that you are the expert, but it is showing people that you are an educator and an advocate for their success.

This is why it is so vitally important that you make your marketing and your content about your prospects and customers, and not about you. You must remind yourself to demonstrate your willingness and ability to share with them and have a genuine concern for their success. That is when they will resonate with you as the authority.

You really should write this down and keep it in front of you for some time until it is second nature.

"I am an educator and an advocate for the success of my prospects and clients."

When you approach content that you create from that mindset, when you create your marketing materials from that mindset, you automatically, and by default, make it about your customers.

One of the easiest exercises to do, one that we do regularly with our own clients, is answer a simple question. If I were to meet you at a party or a networking event and I asked, "What do you do?" – what would that reply sound like?

Almost 90 percent of the time, the reply begins with, "I am" or "I own." I am a chiropractor. I am a fitness instructor. I am a nutritionist. I am a real estate agent. I am a mortgage broker. I own XYZ Company.

When you begin your reply with "I am" or "I own," you can bet on the rest of that conversation being be about you ...

However, if you make a very purposeful effort to begin that reply with "I help," then what you have just done is shifted the momentum to make the rest of that conversation about your prospects and your customers.

So, in the case of a mortgage broker, rather than "I am a mortgage broker" or "I own a mortgage company," it begins with "I help first time home buyers." "I help homeowners reduce their mortgage debt." "I help..." Do you see how that works?

You just made it all about your prospects, their problems, and the solutions that you can provide.

Take some time right now and craft that reply. It doesn't have to be perfect. You do not need to show it to anyone. This is just so that you see in your own mind what a difference it can make being very deliberate about starting your reply with "I help," speaking from the educator and advocate position – making it about them, rather than yourself.

You will quickly see how powerful this can be.

MICRO SPECIALIZATION

Perfection is achieved, not when there is nothing more to add, but when there is nothing left to take away.

Antoine de Saint-Exupery French writer (1900—1944)

Micro Specialization is knowing more about less. It allows you to get more specific about what you are providing, what you are selling, and how you will be seen as an authority for solving problems for your customers and prospects.

It is one of the biggest obstacles that we see our new clients face. Many think it goes against the commonly held logic that more is better. "If I know a little bit, that's great. If I know more, it's better. If I know a lot about a lot of things, even better."

Perfection is not when there is nothing left to add – it's when there is nothing left to take away.

You will find that the less that you focus on, the better you will be able to do what you do, and you will have a more passionate following. People will want to work with you because you are speaking directly to their problem.

For example, consider a general physician who becomes a back specialist. At first, the physician becomes specialized in working on the back. Then as he gets more specialized within his industry, he becomes the doctor that only works with one specific area of the back. Eventually, he gets even more specific about one particular method he uses, and finally, he becomes the expert.

Now, he speaks at conferences and live events, and is a consultant to other doctors and students.

You can see a similar progression in almost any industry. When you see people that are considered an expert in their industry, you will see that they concentrate on a very narrow area of their industry. The experts that can focus on one particular area or aspect are the ones that seem to be the most successful.

Earlier, we discussed individuals such as Dave Ramsey and Richard Simmons who are authorities in their industries. If you look more, you will see that each individual focuses on a specific problem or area within their niche.

Dave Ramsey is a financial authority in the broad sense of the word. He talks about finance, but very rarely does he talk about stocks. He does not talk about the gold index, or bitcoins, or how to invest in real estate. He talks about one thing – getting out of debt. His specialty is just getting out of debt, but he does not focus on every single method for reducing and eliminating debt. He focuses only on a very basic, specialized method.

By narrowing his attention and tightening his area of expertise, he can target a specific audience looking for his solutions to their problems. People that are not in debt have no reason to listen to him, and he does not modify his message to include an audience that is not seeking the solution he provides.

Casting the widest net possible will not position you as an Authority. It will end up diluting your message.

In the quest for expert status or authority status, people sometimes try to be the "I'll do everything and anything" expert. One example is restaurant owners. They produce a menu that has barbecue sandwiches, tacos, pasta and everything in between hoping to offer something for everyone. Eventually, quantity supercedes quality and customers start to wonder: they can make all this stuff, but can they make any of it *well*?

Another example is real estate agents. Real estate agents are notoriously bad marketers in that they try to cast that wide net. Ask a real estate agent who their ideal customer is, and more often than not they will answer: "Everyone! I want to help buyers *and* sellers."

Real estate agents will post a glamour photo of themselves on expensive billboards and shopping carts with ads that say something like "I'm the people's agent."

Well, what is that?

In reality, if they narrowed down their audience, if they said "I'm going to specialize in working with first-time home buyers," or "I'm going to work with empty nesters that are moving on and need to sell their house," then they will have a much better chance at securing those clients.

Agents can easily position themselves as that educator and advocate for the success of their clients and prospects when they can speak to a very specific problem.

In fact, when professionals in any field speak to the problems of a very narrow section of their prospects, they have more success, even though they may be neglecting ninety percent of the potential market by not diluting their message.

Yet another example is a home remodeler that will not remodel just any home. He will only work with real estate investors that want to flip a house, or landlords needing to get their investment properties ready to rent.

Those are the only customers he works for and the only audience he markets to. He does not need to, or want to, work with people that are currently living in the house being remodeled. He works in empty houses where people are not emotionally attached to what he is doing.

Because he only does remodeling for real estate investors, he turns down more work than he takes because his clients are buying the result of working with someone that specializes in their area of need.

"Okay, how do I decide what kind of area I want to work in?"

There are some basic guidelines to help narrow down an area that applies to just about any industry.

First, define your industry or your knowledge base at the very highest level. For instance, if your industry is online marketing, you are helping people market their businesses online. But then you break it down to more specific areas by creating about five different sub-categories for your field. These should be five specific types of prospects that you are willing to work with. Write down some examples and consider them using the SPAN Method.

SPAN: Specific, Pain, Attainable, Numbers

The SPAN method is a four-step process that lets you quickly analyze the earning potential of a niche demand in your industry.

S — Specific Subtopics of Each One (use Google suggested search for ideas).

P — Pain...what specific pains would your topics help alleviate?

A — Attainable...can YOU really help them.

N — Numbers...is there enough of a market to warrant you entering it? Check for competition, Facebook groups, LinkedIn groups, etc.

S is for Specific...

Create specific sub-topics of each category. Then, use Google suggestions to search for ideas.

Suppose a website was recovering from Google penalties. If you do a Google search for that term and scroll down to the bottom of the page, you will see some related topics. If there is more content, you will see more topics.

Don't focus on something so narrow and specialized that it will cause you to run out of content very quickly. You want to be able to provide a variety of solutions to your customers and prospects.

P is for Pain...

Outline the specific pains that your solutions can help alleviate. Don't include only what you think people want, include solutions they need to address their pains.

Show that your offering can take the client's pain away. Consider a point made by Joel Osteen, that if you think back in your life, you can probably remember a time that you've lost something. If you lost twenty bucks, you probably agonized over it for days.

But, if you find twenty bucks in your pocket or in a seat cushion or on the floor or somewhere, you spend it, and you forget about it. It's gone.

That's because we as humans tend to focus on the negative. Make sure you can help people alleviate pain.

Something you will learn from working with doctors is that cures sell better than prevention. People will not buy prevention – they will buy cures.

Who do you think makes more money: the people that sell anti-virus software to prevent viruses, or the people that sell services to recover lost data?

Ensure that your product or service relieves pain. Consider the albino guinea pigs: they would not pass the pain test because while it's nice having a pet, we suspect, it's not a pain thing.

The pain aspect of having an albino guinea pig would be having this pet and not being able to find a vet that is skilled to care for it. Does your vet specialize in dealing with albino guinea pigs? Is there an emergency vet for weekends? List some possible pain points involved and then you can address them.

A is for Attainable...

Make sure you can really provide the products or services you offer to help your customer. Be honest with yourself and do not commit to do something because it sounds cool or it seems easy because somebody else is doing it already.

Look around and you will see "experts" that bounce around from topic to topic. One day, someone is a Facebook expert, then a couple months later they are offering a coaching program on another topic. Then something else starts working, so they change focus again and again.

There is really no way you can help others if you cannot define a problem and focus on solutions. Be honest with yourself, because if you know you cannot make this work, then you cannot help others.

N is for Numbers...

Once you discover that your solution is attainable, be sure that there is a market for your narrow specialty.

So how would you do that?

Facebook is one method. Most people are on Facebook. Search to see how many Facebook groups exist for your niche, your market, or your field. Look at each group and see how big they are.

Facebook pages are also a great indicator: How many Likes do they have? How interactive is this group?

LinkedIn and other industry websites and forums are excellent resources to help you with your market research.

Use the SPAN method since it is a proven process that can help you make an informed decision. Apply any ideas you have right now to this method. Did your idea work within each step of the SPAN method? If so, you know you can focus on the ideas that have real potential and eliminate the bad bets.

The SPAN method will help you focus on a smaller subset of prospects that are your target audience, your most valuable clients.

Howard Stern is probably one of the highest paid media personalities, and hated by around ninety percent of the population. They won't listen to him. But he only needs to focus on the ten percent that gets him, that ten percent that likes him, that ten percent is passionate about him, and they make him rich.

In the car industry, they use a specific model to design cars. They need at least a third of the population to strongly dislike the model. There must be something about the design of the vehicle that rubs some people the wrong way.

They want a third of the population to be passionate about it, to really like it, and to buy it.

Then, they need a third of the population to feel indifferent about the design. These customers neither love nor hate the vehicle.

If you try to cover the field and make a car that does not turn anyone off, then you don't have a remarkable car, because you have set your sights on designing average cars for indifferent drivers.

Consider Ferraris and Lamborghinis and you will find that there are a lot of people that wouldn't drive either one. They don't like the design or they don't care for flashy sports cars in general. But the people that do like those types of cars will pay a lot of money for one.

With this approach, you don't have to compete on price. If price is why customers chose you, it's also why they will choose someone else with a better price. There is always some fool who is willing to offer a lower price and eventually go out of business.

A great brand is not worried about getting paid by every possible person who is willing to pay them. They would prefer to educate and inform the people that they *want* to work with.

So, who do we get to work with? We get to work with those who are looking for real solutions and strategic partners for their long-term success.

INSIDE THE MIND
OF YOUR PROSPECTS

What if you had a crystal ball? Or perhaps even if your prospects just *felt* you had a crystal ball? One that lets you know exactly what they are thinking and feeling, and the outcome they want to achieve.

This is exactly what makes the business celebrities the perceived authorities in the eyes of their daily audience. Somehow knowing what is going on inside their prospect's

mind allows them to resonate so easily and instantly puts them in the position of the educator and advocate for their success because they are speaking directly to them.

Many entrepreneurs try to cast a wide net, and what that does is dilute the power and effectiveness of their message, regardless of how helpful it may be.

When you really understand your prospects and the value of your products and services, then you can craft a riveting message that speaks to their needs. It doesn't matter whether you are using direct mail, your website, video content, radio/TV interviews, or press releases. You will then be seen as an authority without calling yourself an authority or expert. You have now become an advocate for their success.

So how do we do this?

In order to develop your crystal ball there are really just a few questions that you have to ask yourself: Who are my prospects? Who are the people that need and want the help that I can provide?

You also need to ask: What are the common questions my prospects have?

It is amazing to realize how many entrepreneurs can't quickly list the important questions their prospects have. Simply anticipating these questions is a huge advantage and puts you in an authority position.

Then...

What are the perceived obstacles that they have? So many people excuse themselves from an opportunity, so many people excuse themselves from a product or service because they perceive that there is an obstacle there. You have the ability to help them avoid this disservice to themselves.

Almost everyone has some prospects and clients that thought something was going to be a huge deal, a huge obstacle, and it was really nothing. What are those perceived obstacles your clients and prospects have?

Why would they not want to find out about your product or service? Why would they not want to find out more about what you have to offer?

Usually you are inclined to talk about all the reasons a prospect will be interested in your product or service.

Understanding their perceived obstacles and objections

might seem like a backwards approach. Yet, when you understand these issues and are prepared, you can more easily move past them to the benefits and become a success advocate. Put your crystal ball to use and understand the needs and obstacles of your prospects.

Who are my prospects?

To answer this question, let's use a mortgage company as an example. You will then see how to apply it to your industry.

So here's how it typically goes:
Question: Who are my prospects?
Answer: Well...anyone that needs a mortgage.

Wrong answer. You cannot develop a crystal ball with that wide of a net. You have to dig deeper.

A mortgage company's target prospects are first-time home buyers, home buyers who need or want to refinance a home, buyers that have great credit so they are shopping for the best rate. These are the target prospects you should focus on. By narrowing your focus, you are aiming for the bull's eye.

Perhaps you have solutions for buyers that don't have good credit. You would speak to each one of these types of prospects much differently, but so many people try to cast a wide net out there and do not change the way they talk to each of their prospects. It really dilutes the message.

Consider this situation. You are a mortgage broker or loan officer and are meeting someone in person. Before you start telling them what you have to offer, wouldn't you first find out more about them and the situation they might be in?

How could you apply this to other industries? Maybe you are a business coach. What are the situations and the types of people that can use your service? Who is it that you can help?

Determine who you can help and how you can help them. Then craft the main points of a conversation as if you are being interviewed or putting out press releases. Think about who your most valuable prospect is, the one that you have a real passion for helping. That is who you want to speak to.

This does not mean you need to neglect other services or products. What it does mean is that you can do it for each one of those, but you are going to be far more effective if you can narrow it down and speak individually to these prospects.

Oftentimes what happens is that you find one particular prospect that you really do have a passion to help, and you are able to help them significantly, and that becomes the bulk of your business to the extent that you do not really need many (or any) other prospects.

The Four Issues

When your prospect is ready to engage, they always have four issues on their mind. If you have focused your crystal ball strategy, your authority perception will become more apparent and you are in a much better position to convert the prospect into a customer.

Keep in mind that these are issues and questions that your prospects will never ever pick up the phone and call you to ask.

They will never ask these questions in an email. These questions are always on their mind. Your perceived authority will rise significantly if you are able to answer these questions without them ever asking.

They will often come to the wrong conclusions if these unstated questions are not addressed and you might lose the sale. To avoid this, you should address these and get them out of the way. It is really surprising how many different businesses (even coaches & speakers) neglect to address these issues.

Phenomenal success awaits those who understand and address these questions because they are perceived as the authority with the crystal ball.

These are the unspoken questions on the mind of your prospects:

Question #1: Do they understand my problem?

Question #2: Are they qualified to solve my problem?

Question #3: My problem is unique. My problem is different. Will this work for me?

Question #4: What is my risk to find out more? What is my obligation? What am I on the hook for if I dig deeper? Should I do more research before I make contact?

Your prospects want these questions addressed, whether they are addressed by what they find in your marketing or your message. Here is the dangerous part: if you do not address these issues, your prospects will most likely fill in the blanks themselves and the answers they come up with will probably not be to your advantage.

Addressing These Issues

How are we going to do this? We want to *address* these issues without necessarily resolving them all at once. We are going to open up an interactive loop of authority.

Consider just about any soap opera or dramatic TV series where they always leave you hanging at the end. What happens is they always leave things unresolved to make you absolutely nuts to come back next week to find out what happens. That is what we want to do. We want to create that open loop in a lot of our content and the way that we speak.

We want to provide just enough of the right information to entice them to find out more. We want to facilitate interaction.

These are the three strategies we want in our messages, whether the website, video, press releases, direct mail, Facebook posts, LinkedIn posts, or any other form of communication. Creating curiosity, anxiety, and desire will help move the discussion forward.

How do we do this? We do it by addressing, but not answering these questions: Do they understand my problem? Are they qualified to solve my problem? My problem is unique; will this work? What is my risk to find out more?

We are going to address these questions without answering them. Once you see how we are going to do this, it will make complete sense.

Let's start with the first question: "**Do they understand my problem?**" Let's say you are speaking to a first-time home buyer. What are the problems they are faced with? If your niche is the fitness industry, you might be focused on someone who is middle aged, was once in shape, and now needs to get back in shape. Build a picture around that type of person. Do you begin to see how this can be done for your business or industry?

The second question is: "**Are they qualified to solve my problem?**" The temptation is to trot out your resume. "Qualified? Heck yes, I'm qualified. I have these degrees, am certified in this, have this many years of experience, was honored with this, was named #1 in this, was President of this, etc..."

Avoid the resume approach! Instead, focus on them and how you can and have solved problems similar to theirs. You can still weave your qualifications in as you illustrate how others have benefited from your solutions.

Even when it is about you, make it about them. How many years have you worked in your current industry? How many prospects with similar problems have you helped in the past?

For example, if you want to work with dentists and have experience in that field, how many years? How many dentists and dental practices have you helped?

These are the two numbers you need to come up with for now. That's it! Forget about degrees and certifications for now.

Let's turn our attention to the third question: "**My problem is unique; will this work?**" We have all seen and asked this question. Everyone always feels that their problem is unique, that it might have worked for others, but it won't work for them. This question is very common and we have all used it.

When you consider these problems that people think are unique only to them, start the sentence with "Even if..."

For the mortgage company it could be: "Even if you've had credit problems in the past or have recently changed jobs..." For the business coach, it could be: "Even if you have not secured your first client..."

You want them to feel that (1) their situation might not be as unique as they think it is, or (2) you are experienced at dealing with unique situations.

Therefore, for any niche that you want to target, try to understand why they will think their problems are unique. Then use the "Even if..." in front of those statements. It will become easier for them to think: "Oh well, maybe my situation is not so unique after all." At that point they will be more receptive to listen to your proposals.

The last question is: "**What is my risk to find out more?**" The Law of Reciprocity governs much of our social interactions. When someone takes time to work with us or does us a favor, we tend to feel obligated to respond in kind. Allowing this interaction to take place can be perceived as a risk, especially if we are not sure that we will be able to return the favor. It might not be a financial risk. It could be: "If I go one step further, have I obligated myself to keep going?"

Consider the marketing tactics often associated with timeshares. Have you ever been invited to a timeshare presentation and did not go? Even though they said there was no obligation to purchase, all you had to do was sit through a presentation to receive a free weekend at their resort property. Free, are you kidding me? Many people won't go because they will feel obligated to take the full tour and then listen to a high pressure sales pitch after the initial presentation. Some people won't feel obligated. Yet, a lot of people will and they would rather avoid that obligation instead of seeing if the free weekend is for real.

We need to remove all unnecessary obstacles that would stand in the way of prospects and clients to contact you. By being an educator and advocate for their success, they will feel like they need to find out more.

Phrases like "free consultation" can evoke feelings of obligation, since many consider this as "bait". Free is a word that invokes a fear that we are going to be obligated. If we go in for a free consultation, we will have put them to work. We made them engage and now we are going to feel obligated to go farther that we are comfortable. Right?

Be very careful about what you think is a valuable proposition and understand that their fear of obligation may be stronger than their fear of monetary cost.

How do we tie all of this together?

Make this conversational. Remove the corporate speak from your dialog. Do not throw in power words. "Do you want to take your business to the next level? Do you want to leverage your business?" Always make the conversation about the customer.

If someone is struggling in their business, they may not be ready when you ask them to take their business to the next level. "I'm not ready for that! I just want to get my business going!" Do not give them reasons to excuse themselves by using corporate speak.

Speak directly to your prospects. You will have far more success this way.

If you listen to people that are positioned as authorities, Dave Ramsey for instance, he does not use financial speak. He speaks to the audience, to his prospects.

Speak the language of your prospect. Do not try to sound more clever than them or smarter than them. Do not use a language that is different than the way that they would speak. Speak the language of your prospect.

You need to make your prospect think: "Wow, maybe they do understand my problem, and they seem to be qualified to solve it. Maybe my problem isn't that unique, and if it is, they seem to be able to deal with unique problems. There's really no reason for me not to check this out."

When you address these four issues with purpose, not answers, but purpose, you are going to find it changes their perception of you. You are going to find it changes the way that you speak to your prospects and your clients, and it positions you as an educator and advocate for their success.

How do we apply this with Authority?

You can apply this to many elements of your business: writing copy for a landing page, creating a script for an opt-in video, writing a description for your book, providing talking points or questions for radio, podcasts, TV interviews or press releases.

When you go through the exercise of thinking about your prospect, narrowing it down to that one person's problem, and figuring out how to address those four issues, you are going to quickly be able to speak as an authority. You will be able to create that anxiety and curiosity so that they will want to know more from you.

Let's say we're doing an opt-in video for this mortgage company. Here's how we can apply what we just went over.

"Hi, I'm John Smith, President of Acme Mortgage. If you are a first-time home buyer you probably have a lot of questions. How much down payment do I need? What kind of credit score is required? How much house can I afford?"

Make them feel that maybe you *do* understand their problem.

Let's move on to Scene 2.

"At Acme Mortgage we've helped hundreds of families finance their first home and I'm confident that we can help you."

That simple statement addresses the question of "Are they qualified to solve my problem?" There is no need to have your resume here, you have already stated you are experienced with different problems.

But isn't my problem unique?

"Even if you've had some credit bruises in the past or just started a new job you may be surprised at the options available."

Now they are thinking: "Hmmm, maybe my problem isn't that unique, and if it is, then maybe they're used to dealing with unique problems."

Finally, "I'd like to invite you to get a free, no obligation, evaluation so that you can see just how Acme Mortgage can help you finance your first dream home."

You have now given them no reason to dig further. You created curiosity because you did not answer any of the questions, but acknowledged them and addressed them. Now they are thinking: "Yes, I think they understand my problem. I feel they're qualified. My problem may not be that unique and I really have no risk to find out more."

This is how we create curiosity, anxiety, and the desire for them to step further and get closer to understand how our solutions can help them. We have made the opportunity to communicate deeper with them and find out more about their specific situation, which is exactly what we want to do.

We want to make them feel that we understand, that we are willing to educate them, that we are an advocate, truly concerned about their success, and we need to make them comfortable enough to want to find out more.

You can get laser focused on their specific problem when they do come to find out more. When trying to present authority, too many people feel that they need to give every credential and scenario. They overload people with information to try to prove they are an expert.

Unfortunately, as you try to paint an all-inclusive picture by giving more information, you give people more reasons to excuse themselves from the offer. There is no way that you can portray a complete picture that will satisfy *every* prospect. Painting a full picture for one prospect will make another person excuse themselves because: "Oh, well, see? That's not going to work for me."

Give them just enough information to allow them to paint their own picture of the results that they feel they can get from working with you. It is going to be a far better and a more accurate picture for them.

This is how you get inside the mind of your prospect with authority; not by providing more information but by providing just enough

- to generate that curiosity, anxiety and desire to want to find out more about you,
- to understand that you are someone that does care about their success,
- to realize that you do have the information that they need to make a decision on how to move forward.

Go through these exercises and apply them to your Industry.

You will quickly see how you can get laser focused. When you get inside the mind of your customer, there is never a need for you to call yourself the expert... but you are giving *them* every reason to.

THE FOUR FACES – YOUR AUTHORITY AVATAR

When people are looking to experts, the authority, what they really want is to be able to identify with leaders. They may want these leaders to have the attributes or the qualities that they want to achieve. They sometimes want the expert to have the attributes or qualities that they already recognize in themselves.

Think about it. A lot of people really do admire others that have qualities they recognize within themselves, as well as attributes or qualities that instill confidence in that authority's ability to solve their problem. That is one of the most important things that people look for when they start to follow an authority.

What if they want their leader to possess qualities that they feel they themselves could never achieve? Your Authority Avatar is something you should carefully consider before you make a big mistake in communicating with your prospects in a way that may actually push them away without you even knowing why.

Creating and developing your authority avatar, your authority persona, is very important to your positioning and ability to connect with your prospects.

You are not going to create a completely different character from whom you are. It should be an extension of your natural personality.

Be purposeful in the message, in how you make people feel about you, in the way that you create content, and even with the language that you use.

The core of your authority avatar is, of course, the educator and advocate. You will build your persona on top of that.

Most people will naturally fall into one of four main categories when creating and developing their persona.

We call these the Four Faces of Authority

1. **Joe Everyman**. This is the "If They Can Do It Then I Can Do It Too" authority persona.
2. **The Cowboy**. This is the No B.S. straight shooter authority persona.
3. **The Soldier.** This is the defender authority persona.
4. **The Wizard**. The magician avatar.

The next section discusses each one of these so that you can clearly identify which one you associate with. You will see that it really is a very natural process.

JOE EVERYMAN

IF THEY CAN DO IT, I CAN DO IT AUTHORITY

The Joe Everyman persona is "If He or She Can Do It Then I Can Do It Too." People identify with this authority avatar as someone having a similar quality, but also similar flaws, as themselves. This authority is definitely not perfect and has battle scars from dealing with their own obstacles. People identify with this authority, flaws and all, because they have overcome something.

This authority cannot want to be the smartest person in the room. This is a very important point. We have seen this as being one of the biggest obstacles that several of our clients have had to overcome.

Many often feel that if they want to be seen as the expert they have to also be seen as the smartest person in the room. They have to be seen as having some kind of special intelligence or being extra clever or having some kind of special ability in order to be seen as the expert. What they find is that this can actually be very counterproductive and detrimental to the authority persona and hurt the connection and relationship with their prospects.

The power of the Joe Everyman avatar is that they aren't so different from anyone else. They just happened to have discovered a way to succeed. Do you see how that may conflict with being the smartest person in the room?

The "If He or She Can Do It Then I Can Do It Too" attraction is based upon the fact that this person found a path to success, whether it was business, relationships, finance, or whatever it may be. They found that path to success and now they're bringing back the map for others like them to be able to follow.

Jared, from the Subway commercials, is a great example. Like many, he was overweight and obese, yet he didn't give up. The only difference is that Jared overcame those issues, and that's why people looked to him as an inspiration, an authority, as someone to help guide them. People saw him as finding the path to losing weight by eating Subway sandwiches. He was bringing back the map to show them how they could do it as well.

The Joe Everyman Authority is very well suited for coaching, business start-ups or money management. If you are a coach, selling info products, how-to information or systems, weight loss, or fitness, then your audience would most likely connect with this persona. Think about some of the most successful fitness coaches. Many once had serious issues with weight, health and fitness. People see them as someone that overcame those issues and it helps them feel that they can do that as well.

With this Authority avatar, people see the authority as someone that's not much different than them, someone with the same problems, issues and challenges, yet they were able to overcome them. That's a very powerful persona to have.

Maybe that's the persona that fits you as most aligned with your natural personality. However if it's not, you probably don't want to force yourself into that avatar.

CELEBRITY EXAMPLES:
Jared from Subway, Chris Gardner, Rocky Balboa, Rudy Ruettiger

THE COWBOY

NO B.S. AUTHORITY

The Cowboy authority persona can be very compelling *because* it often makes people uncomfortable. Making others uncomfortable with this No B.S. avatar is not a bad thing and can be quite a powerful position when your audience is likely to connect with someone who is tough and firm, but still compassionate.

You can probably think of some Cowboy business celebrities in your industry right now. The No B.S. authority strengthens the trust of prospects by concurring with their hesitations and their doubts, but then giving them rational and realistic solutions.

Let's use weight loss again. The Cowboys are the ones saying: "Of course you haven't lost weight. Of course you lose weight and then you gain it back. Of course you do, because it's hard to have will power and hard to not eat the stuff you want." They're saying things that go against what you've heard before. If others say it's easy then the Cowboy, No B.S. persona is saying: "Well, of course they *say* it's easy. It isn't easy, but there is a way."

Then they give a rational and logical solution to a realistic approach that can work. This avatar may or may not be the smartest person in the room, but they have the guts to say what everyone else is thinking. Think about celebrity Cowboy authorities like Jim Cramer, Gary Vaynerchuk or Larry Winget.

These No B.S. personas are very bold and brash and tell it like it is. There's usually no spoonful of sugar to help the medicine go down.

Prospects that resonate with this avatar may feel like they

lack discipline to succeed because they have always fallen for easy answers. They want someone who is going to whip them into shape.

This persona works well in fitness and nutrition, which is why people hire personal trainers that are going to push them further than they could push themselves. They want accountability.

The Cowboy avatar works well with how-to products. I'm sure you've heard "The No B.S. way to X, Y, & Z."

People want a No B.S. coach that will tell them when they are wrong. They are not going to be yes men. They are going to give their clients the real, straight answers.

If this is your persona, chances are you recognized it early in this section. Remember, it is not about creating a new personality, it's an extension of who you are naturally.

CELEBRITY EXAMPLES:
Jim Cramer, Larry Winget, Gary Vaynerchuk, Grant Cardone, Han Solo

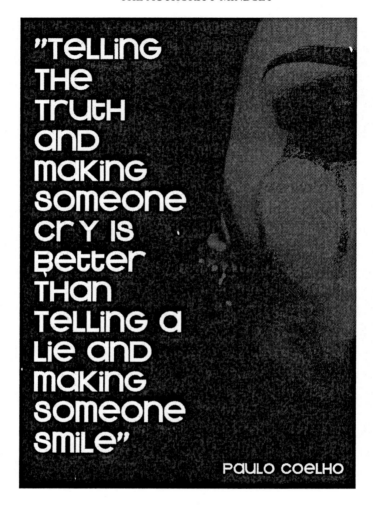

THE SOLDIER

DEFENDER AUTHORITY

The Soldier is an authority avatar that can be extremely effective especially when it is very tightly aligned with your natural authentic self. The Soldier is someone that has knowledge, the willingness and the ability to make problems go away.

They are a natural defender. They can make good things happen. They can steer prospects and customers in the right direction while avoiding pitfalls.

The Soldier can instill confidence and is sometimes perceived as the smartest person in the room, and that's okay. Think about celebrity experts like Dave Ramsey or Suze Orman. Customers or the prospects that feel overwhelmed or defenseless are the types of prospects that connect with this defender.

This persona works very well in many areas such as finance, alternative medicine, health and wellness, consumer advocates, legal, and anywhere that prospects and customers feel like David versus Goliath underdog.

These professionals come to your defense, such as the attorney defending against the IRS.

They will be saying, "There is a solution and it's not your fault that you don't know what it is."

CELEBRITY EXAMPLES:
Dave Ramsey, Dr. Oz, Suze Orman, Superman

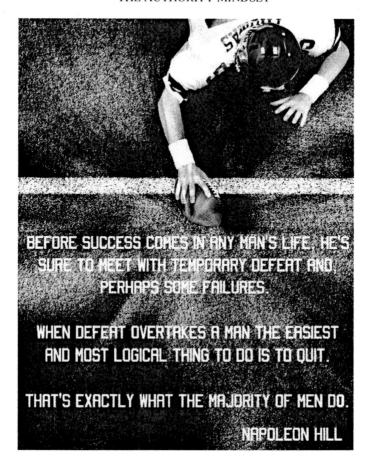

BEFORE SUCCESS COMES IN ANY MAN'S LIFE, HE'S
SURE TO MEET WITH TEMPORARY DEFEAT AND,
PERHAPS SOME FAILURES.

WHEN DEFEAT OVERTAKES A MAN THE EASIEST
AND MOST LOGICAL THING TO DO IS TO QUIT.

THAT'S EXACTLY WHAT THE MAJORITY OF MEN DO.

NAPOLEON HILL

THE WIZARD

Now The Wizard is a persona that few should take on. However, so many mistakenly feel they need to have prospects and customers perceive them as the smartest person in the room. The Wizard has specialized knowledge and powers. The Wizard can do things that the average person cannot do.

The Wizard avatar connects very strongly with customers and prospects that can benefit just by being part of this wizard's world — just by being around them or allowing them to work their magic on the prospect's problem. The Wizard is often perceived as the smartest or most gifted person in the room.

If you think about Wizard avatars or personas, think about people like Tony Robbins, innovators like Steve Jobs, or inspirational speakers like Joel Olsteen. These are personalities that have achieved a level of authority and produce results that your average person wouldn't feel they could attain themselves.

The prospect feels that they benefit by being part of that wizard's world. They benefit by being surrounded by that wizard's energy or knowledge and that can be very alluring to a lot of people when developing their authority avatar. They want to be seen as that wizard, but it can backfire if it does not match up with your prospects.

The Wizard works well with people that are inspirational speakers, consultants, or medical specialists. Prospects resonate with this avatar just by letting them work their magic on the problem.

They are considered to have some sort of special knowledge,

skill or gift.

CELEBRITY EXAMPLES:
Tony Robbins, Joel Osteen, Oprah Winfrey, Steve Jobs, Bruce Lee

WHICH AUTHORITY PERSONA ARE YOU?

So which authority persona are you? What is the product or solution you provide? Is it coaching, consulting, information, how-to products? Is it Done For You services, physical products? Let's look at some examples.

Coaching – If you are a coach, chances are you are going to be okay being the Joe Everyman, Cowboy or Soldier.

The Wizard, however, can present challenges. If your prospects feel that you have some kind of special gift or talent, or an advantage to gaining your position, they may not feel that they can achieve those results themselves. They may feel like "Oh, well, that's why he or she is successful. I don't have that so it won't work for me." You have to be extremely careful about that.

Consulting – You must be careful about taking on the Joe Everyman avatar here. If you are a consultant and people are hiring you to come in and do things for them or implement systems, do you really want them to think "Well, gosh, if this person can do this there's no reason we can't do it."

You can certainly be The Cowboy. You can be The Soldier. You can even be The Wizard. Those work really well for consulting because people want consultants to have some special talent or some special knowledge that they do not have or could easily attain. They usually do not want to know how it works, they just want the consultant to make it work.

Selling Information, How-to Products or Training – The Joe Everyman is certainly a great avatar. You want your prospects to feel very much that they can do it.

The No B.S. Cowboy avatar who cuts to the chase and shows

you exactly how it is done works nicely as well. The Soldier can work in this area, although a lot of times people see The Soldier as that defender that will be with them each step of the way giving them strength and helping them over the obstacles that they cannot get past on their own.

The Wizard can be tough as well. People may find that they won't have the ability to implement wizard information if it's a how-to type product. For example, the Queen of England would not do well selling information on "How To Be The Queen of England" because most people realize that there's no amount of information that will allow them to achieve that. They're not going to be the Queen of England no matter how hard they try or how much knowledge they acquire.

Done For You Services – The Joe Everyman can work sometimes. It really depends on what you are providing. Services like changing oil or mowing lawns might be services you would pay someone to do even though you could certainly do them if you wanted to. This rarely works with high value services.

The Cowboy and The Soldier work well. Even the Wizard avatar works for services and anything that's done-for-you.

What About Combining Two Avatars? We have clients that often say "you know, I kind of see myself as a crossover between the Joe Everyman and the Cowboy." That's ok. You may have attributes of a combination of these that can easily blend together if it fits with the audience and prospects that you are working with.

Don't ever try to combine Joe Everyman and the Wizard, since we have never seen it work. In fact, we have seen it be the downfall of some really talented entrepreneurs. For lack of a better way of putting it, the self-esteem of Joe Everyman is not the same as for the Wizard and this will put you in a dangerous conflicted position.

When people resonate with the "If He or She Can Do It Then I Can, Too," they want to feel that that person has the same flaws, the same challenges, and overcame the same types of obstacles. Prospects will immediately lose that connection if they feel that authority had a special talent or gift, or were given a privileged situation in order to make that happen. It just doesn't work.

So be very careful about feeling like you need to be the smartest person in the room or imply that you have some special advantage if your audience really needs the Joe Everyman.

NEXT STEPS

Now that you have a better understanding of the Authority Mindset and the types of Authority personas that exist, you are ready to claim your Authority. Remember, being an Authority is not about you telling everyone that you are the expert – it is about others saying it for you.

For others to talk about you, they need to know about you. Below are some steps you can take to show your prospects and customers that you are an Educator and Advocate for their success.

Get Your First Speaking Gig

Speaking gigs create multiple opportunities. First, they allow you to get hot prospects or leads. Second, you could get so many speaking engagements that you could become one of the highest paid speakers in your field. Finally, they help you to successfully build your brand. All of this translates into growth for your business.

Of course, the key to achieving these favorable results is to actually get invited to do a speaking engagement. So what do you do? Try these three important steps on how to get your first speaking gig.

1. Establish Your Niche Audience

Start with knowing your niche audience. This is an important consideration because you can better make your presence felt and establish your relevance in the lives of those who actually care about the information that you hold and can share.

If you make it known that you are an authority and a good repository of knowledge, customers and prospects will seek you out. Then, you can offer to present all the information you have through a speaking gig. The key here is to turn the offer into your opportunity for a speaking gig.

2. Keep Learning and Be the Best Speaker in Your Field

Seminars and workshops can get lifeless, especially when they run too long, with little to no insight from speakers. So, it is important for you to keep learning and adding to your knowledge base. Pursuing knowledge is particularly critical when you are consulting in fields that continue to evolve, such as technology and marketing.

Being the best speaker involves much more than presenting the latest relevant information. To hold your audience's interest, you need to hone your speaking skills, study voice projection, gestures, and some acting. It's important to get the gestures and the voice projection just right for the specific audience and to use adequate tools to maintain their attention. By improving your public speaking skills, you can become a more dynamic and engaging speaker. You will then get your message across more effectively. Join a local Toastmasters club for a very supportive environment to enhance your speaking skills.

3. Use the Web to Create Interest and to Market Your Expertise

The great thing about attracting speaking engagements these days is that you don't have to invest a great amount of money on marketing yourself. The Web offers multiple opportunities for gaining exposure. You have webinars, podcasts, Google Hangouts and YouTube videos; these are all speaking engagements that you can offer like products. Create a website as well to interact with your target market. Determine the topics that interest your audience so you can create an event for those to be discussed.

Each one will not only create interest in you as an expert in your field, but also showcase your engaging approach to talking and presenting certain subjects.

And before you know it, you'll be getting that invite for your first traditional speaking gig.

Get Your Business on Local News

One good way to increase brand awareness is by being featured in the news. Many people still get their community information from the local news, so it's always effective for a company to direct attention to their business by coming out on the local news.

However, news stations need to make sure that businesses offer something interesting, relevant, and newsworthy. Just being that reliable business establishment in the community is not enough.

To get your business on local news, get your community interested, and share more about your operations, here are some effective and easy tactics to try.

1. Build Relationships

Connect on Twitter, Facebook, LinkedIn and Instagram with

the reporters you plan on pitching. Compliment the reporter on these social channels publicly. Share their stories and tag them with hashtags.

2. Support Your Community

Take a cue from the local juice place or bakery that helps sponsor community events that normally get featured on the news. These events really look for sponsors, whether they are SEO companies that can help market the event and really just spread the news, or the neighborhood pub where participants of the event can get a discount on some chow. Your business may not get a full feature, but it will likely appear when the event is reported on the news. This is a great starting point to make contacts with producers too.

3. Hold a "Free for All" Event for Your Business With Recognizable Personalities

Anything that gathers a lot of people together and also has distinguishable personalities present easily becomes newsworthy.

4. Ask Your Local Radio Station About Live Remote Broadcasts

Get the local radio stations involved as well. This is very effective, just tie the broadcast in with a special event, contest or free offer.

The DJs can promote your event on air, and they can really make it so much more fun for everybody.

5. Support Your Local News Stations

Offer some of your products or services for free or at greatly discounted rates. Cupcake shops all around the country have tried this tactic, especially for morning news shows. At first the businesses just get a "thank you" on air, then later on they get featured for reports on food and popular interests. This tactic is very effective in fostering beneficial relationships with members of the media.

6. Be a Reliable Source for Your Field and Available For Interviews

This is a great way to get media coverage for your business. If reporters come asking for help regarding the stories they wish to present, don't ever be too busy to accommodate them. It's good to build a relationship because this can lead to a full feature -- especially if you prove yourself to be a reliable expert in your field of business.

Write a Book

One of the best ways to position yourself is to author a book. A book is the ultimate brochure — it promotes your services and business and gets you free publicity. But most importantly, it makes you stick out among your competitors as the Authority.

Get Featured in News Articles

Always keep your business, product, or service in the spotlight. Be sure to promote any newsworthy event, such as a local radio interview or participation in a charity event, through a News Release. If you publish a book, be sure to follow up with a News Release. If your book reaches Best Seller status, share that in a News Release as well.

If you are unsure about how to get started with News Releases or Articles, try helpareporter.com (HARO). This service enables journalists to connect with people who are experts, or Authorities, in a particular niche. The journalist can interview you as an expert and quote you as the expert in the interview in a niche article.

Contact an Authority Marketing Professional to do it For You

There is nothing wrong with asking for help. As we discussed earlier, many people feel they are just a few steps away from becoming an Authority and want to wait to claim that title. In most cases, however, those people are already Authorities. They just don't realize it.

An Authority Marketing Professional can quickly put you on the path to become an Authority. Allowing someone else to point you in the right direction will remove the roadblocks that are preventing you from claiming your Authority.

PROFILES OF AUTHORITY

Behind the Marketing Minds of the Contributing Authors

DAVID BAME, JR.

BUSINESS: Bullseye Marketing Agency, LLC

WEBSITE: 321Bullseye.com

EMAIL: David@321Bullseye.com

LOCATION: Bainbridge, New York

FACEBOOK: Facebook.com/david.bame.71

Marketing Director, David Bame, Jr., Owner of Bullseye Marketing Agency, LLC was a self-starting entrepreneur from a very young age. "I was brought up in a family of modest means — if you wanted more than the basics you needed to find something you could do that you could earn some money doing."

"I always knew I wanted to do something productive with my time and my life," he adds, "Not to mention there were no 'Help Wanted' posters for anyone under 16 so you had to create your own job if you wanted money." Between 12 and 13 years old Bame started a lawn mowing business. He was able to borrow start-up money for equipment after explaining the business plan to his grandmother. She cut the check and he cut the grass for what became several years of a good little business for Bame.

He added a second business the following year which was a flower service. He planted several varieties of flowers, cut and arranged them, and sold them at the Farmers Market in town. "It was there that I picked up regular clients including a hotel and a restaurant, but I must say being a young man in school athletics, I took some heat for being the 'Flower Guy'."

The year Bame was 15 he experienced his first entrepreneurial stumble. "I started a trapping business for the Fall and Winter months where I caught muskrats and raccoons and sold the furs. I soon discovered I had serious moral issues with my own business. Right or wrong, I quickly formed the belief that if you're going to take the life of an animal it should be for a better reason than just the money. Taking just the fur was not for me. I sold my traps and closed."

Bame worked as a lifeguard to save up for college, eventually earning a college degree in Business Administration. He worked third shift night auditing for hotels, did some factory work during the day, then he went on to work for the state of New York, after which, he went into sales and marketing for a couple different privately owned companies. Then it was right back to entrepreneurship. "When I worked for other companies after college I felt limited in many ways, especially creatively and innovatively," he says, "I was bored and uninspired. A specific job within a pre-defined job description was too constrictive. I wanted to be able to contribute more."

After further studying and business planning while working for others, Bame committed to charting his own course in business that allowed him the personal freedom to help mankind in the best way he thought he could. It was then that he became a dedicated lifetime entrepreneur marketer.

For the past couple decades Bame has started, built and successfully sold three brick and mortar businesses in different industries. "It has been one heck of a ride and I say that tongue-in-cheek because one of the businesses I built and sold was a limousine livery service," he adds. "Riding around in big super fancy Cadillacs and Lincolns was a heck of a nice ride and creating a lifetime memories for my clients was also very rewarding work. I know that I'm part of hundreds of family and friends' home videos playing the role of the chauffeur."

"The journey from young entrepreneur just starting out to seasoned entrepreneurial veteran began with hope, faith, and belief along with self-determination and a willingness to keep trying no matter how many failures I experienced," Bame says. "I recognize the importance of quickly learning from my failures to minimize them by failing quick and failing forward. I maximize my successes by consistently building upon what I've learned from both failure and success."

According to Bame, practicing good basic business principles and having the desire and mindset of providing as much value as possible to anyone you do business with can help anyone go from aspiring green entrepreneur to one of diverse experience. Cultivating intuitive vision and pursuing ongoing training opportunities also leads to business success.

Bame's company, Bullseye Marketing Agency, LLC, helps other businesses promote themselves by cutting through the confusion of the new digital marketing age to identify the opportunities that will work best for them.

Bame currently helps other businesses find, attract, and convert new customers into new streams of revenue by strategically promoting them in the new world of digital media.

Learn more about David Bame, Jr. and Bullseye Marketing Agency, LLC at: http://www.321Bullseye.com.

NORA BENYAHYA

BUSINESS: Authority Talent Coaching

WEBSITE: AuthorityTalentCoach.com

EMAIL: Nora@AuthorityTalentCoach.com

LOCATION: Kuala Lumpur, Malaysia

FACEBOOK: Facebook.com/profile.php?
id=100008191840316

TWITTER: Twitter.com/norabenyahya

Authority Talent Coach, Nora Benyahya aligns her clients personal and business development needs through her, "Lead to Succeed – Personal and Business Acceleration Coaching Program" to help them unlock their potential and monetize their talents as an authority in their field of expertize.

She first became interested in entrepreneurship when she finished college. "When I was 22, fresh out of college, I got my first job working for a very successful entrepreneur,"

Benyahya explains, "The entrepreneur I worked for had diverse business interests, ranging from consumer products to holiday resorts to automotive dealerships. I learned from observing him, how by being in business I could potentially earn unlimited income, compared to being a salaried employee like I was. I knew then that was the way for me, that I was going to own my own business one day. And sure enough, several years down the road, after climbing the corporate ladder and gaining some experience, I started my first business."

In the year 2000, after being awarded exclusive territory rights to market a popular consumer product brand, Benyahya started her first business. "I wasn't sure if I was going to be successful at it, however, I went to work. I opened up sales channels by appointing sub-agents under me and I did that consistently for six months. And soon after, I started to see my sales rise month after month. I went from making five figure sales a month to six figure sales a month and I did that continuously for four years before I sold my shares to my business partner. That was when it dawned on me that I had become an entrepreneur."
After she left she went on to be a panel consultant for a government backed entrepreneurship program on marketing and branding.

Today Benyahya is a professionally trained authority talent coach. She says, "I help my clients find the gold nuggets in themselves and translate that into their business. I do it through my unique three step process combining business systems experience with talent coaching." First, she assesses their talents and their business with a business growth audit. Then she draws up a personal development plan and a business report for them—like a road map to help them expand their personal competencies to achieve their business growth. Once she's done that successfully, she can position them as an authority in their area of expertise. "This process helps them grow their business a whole lot faster than if they were to do it alone by themselves," she explains.

She has been coaching one on one and led group workshops fulltime for the last four years for various multinationals, SMEs, government agencies and NGOs. She has worked with clients from twelve different countries such as Spain, Germany, Korea, America, Liberia, Canada, Hong Kong, Singapore, Thailand and Indonesia just to name a few. Her versatility makes it easy for her clients to relate to her regardless of their cultural diversity.

In her spare time Benyahya who is also the president of a non-profit organization which advocates underprivileged children's access to education, volunteers her time setting up children literacy classes aptly named New Hope and running fundraising activities with her team. As a nature lover she also counts beekeeping and organic farming as her other hobbies.

Learn more about Authority Talent Coach, Nora Benyahya at: http://www.authoritytalentcoach.com.

JOHN P.BERRY

WEBSITE: Appspertise.com

EMAIL: john@ Appspertise.com

LOCATION: Scottsdale, Arizona

FACEBOOK: Facebook.com/TheJohnBerry

TWITTER: Twitter.com/johnpberry

LINKEDIN: LinkedIn.com/in/jpberry

YOUTUBE: Youtube.com/user/TheJPB

Serial entrepreneur John Berry has had a strong example of the benefits of entrepreneurship since he was young. Berry says, "My mother was and still is very much an entrepreneur; she has always been figuring out ways to make money for herself rather than just working for somebody else."

Berry decided he was going to be an entrepreneur himself when he took a look around and noticed a couple of things.

"I work with a lot of really smart people who are not only not rich (and probably never will be), but don't own their own time. The government takes way too much of my 'income' and I will never be paid what I'm worth if I work for someone else," he explains. He wonders, "If I save and make the company I work for millions every year, why don't I hire me to do the same for my own business?"

There are two notable businesses in Berry's past that define his journey from a green entrepreneur to a seasoned one. Berry's first business was a Ready Mix concrete company and the second was an assisted living company. In both cases, he feels like he made huge mistakes and says he's still paying the price today, both literally and figuratively.

"The concrete venture was supposed to be easy," he says, "I was providing the financing and my partner was supplying the expertise. It just so happened that in the time we went from concept to launch the entire market changed — price of materials skyrocketed, fuel costs went way up, and I could swear a new Ready Mix company popped up in our area every other week."

The assisted living did not go much better. In both cases however, he learned valuable skills with respect to the Internet, online marketing, and real marketing that he uses in his business today.

"I can help any business get more revenue and profit from what they already have. I can spot where there are small gaps and I can spot gaping holes that represent pure opportunity and is effectively free."
That's essentially what large corporations have paid Berry for in the past.

"Do you think you could dominate your market if you had access to the same time tested techniques that Fortune 10 companies are using every single day?" he asks. "There are predators and there are prey, survival goes to the ones that adapt the fastest."

DUSTIN BRILEY

BUSINESS: Yoobly

WEBSITE: Yoobly.com

LOCATION: Phoenix, Arizona

FACEBOOK: Facebook.com/brileydustin

TWITTER: Twitter.com/yoobly

LINKEDIN: LinkedIn.com/in/dustinbriley

Currently I run Yoobly.com & Tattoos.org and have built several multi-million dollar businesses, most of them from scratch.

I founded the first at 20, during college, and ended up generating as high as $80k/month in revenue within the first 3 years. Believe it or not, but that was a house painting business in Alaska – how random is that?!

That business exploded when I figured out marketing.

Were we the best painters in Anchorage? Of course not (I can admit that now).

So if we weren't the best and we didn't grow through word-of-mouth, how did we make $80,000/month in the high season? Because I discovered internet marketing.

The painting business sold for a nice chunk, thanks to our tremendous online reputation – it taught me that today, building an online reputation is your biggest branding task.

But to operate a successful business, lead gen and traffic are your biggest tasks.

And nobody can turn around your lead gen and traffic like me. I'll:

• Develop a kickass strategy.
• Teach you how to achieve it.
• Push you to actually execute.

(Because everyone needs a nudge, sometimes.)

For 15 years, I've been on a constant search for new opportunities, working with other entrepreneurs and pushing the boundaries of what is possible in business. I specialize in network marketing in part because even though it's hard, I know how to make any MLM business explode.

But I'm also open to any challenge.

Let's turn your business around. Together.

To learn more visit: http://www.DustinBriley.com.

TIM CHERMAK

EMAIL: timchermak@gmail.com

LOCATION: Willmar, Minnesota

FACEBOOK: Facebook.com/timchermak

Like many of his friends, Tim Chermak collected baseball cards as a hobby. Looking back, this simple 'childhood hobby' was essential in his development as a marketer and entrepreneur. "I learned many great life lessons by collecting cards," Chermak says. When he was only 7 years old he opened a basic retail business dealing in baseball cards. "This micro-enterprise taught me a valuable lesson early on in life: the business value of having 'expert' status in your niche.

My enterprise was based out of my bedroom, and the store hours were dictated by my parents' willingness to tolerate the neighbor kids stopping by."

"At age 7, my income was a whopping $5/week allowance.

That was just enough to buy one pack of new cards every seven days. Usually this 'inventory' was procured during my mom's weekly trip to our local Target. I proudly tagged along with my $5 bill and a huge smile on my face," Chermak recalls.

Chermak convinced his mom to buy the latest Beckett magazine each month — the standard trade journal for the card collecting industry at the time. In each issue of Beckett, it listed the 'book value' of each card. "I used the Beckett magazine to categorize all of my cards," Chermak explains. "I kept accurate records of the value of my cards. At any given time, I could have quoted you what my collection was worth...down to the individual cards. I just needed to know what my cards were worth, because it gave me an advantage on the trading floor."

"For example," he says, "if my friend Austin wanted to trade me his Chipper Jones rookie card for my Derek Jeter rookie card, I ran the numbers. What was Austin's card worth? What was my card worth? Were there any intangibles involved? Was either player injured? Was their team going to the World Series that year?" Chermak quickly developed authority positioning with the neighborhood kids. They would ask him for advice on potential trades or what brand of cards to buy.

Chermak's business is a little more sophisticated now, but the principles remain the same. The goal is always making sales (and teaching clients how to do the same). Today, he helps real estate professionals establish themselves as experts in their local market by authoring a book.

"At an early age I learned the importance of having expert status. Insider knowledge is both a general business asset and a marketing asset — people want to do business with experts. And there's nothing that can get you to expert, celebrity status quicker than writing a book," Chermak says. "If you can be the rainmaker that delivers paying customers (to your business or someone else's business), you will never have to worry about money."

Just as he learned in his first gig selling baseball cards to his friends, Chermak feels that the key to business is making sales from a position of authority. "The formula is simple," he explains, "publish and promote valuable information that positions you as an authority, and then convert the leads into paying customers. And that's really what authority marketing is all about."

Tim Chermak can be reached at: timchermak@gmail.com.

NOBLE CRAWFORD III

WEBSITE: Noblecrawford.com

EMAIL: noble@noblecrawford.com

LOCATION: Dallas, TX

TWITTER: Twitter.com/noblecrawford

LINKEDIN: LinkedIn.com/in/noblecrawford

Noble Crawford's entry point into entrepreneurialism happened 22 years ago. At that time, he was learning creative design for websites. He soaked up everything that he could find about building web pages, html, CSS and learning how to upload content through FTP. You name it, Crawford consumed it and taught himself how to do it. He was presented with an opportunity to design the very first website for a new non-profit agency called Hope Farm, Inc. (http://www.HopeFarmInc.org).

Crawford was able to design and host the website for Hope Farm, Inc. and while working on their project became a website hosting reseller. To become a reseller he needed to create a business, later he used that same business as a platform for offering web design services. Hope Farm, Inc. was Crawford's very first customer and he gained additional customers after completing that first job. According to Crawford, that was his first taste of entrepreneurialism.

He got his feet wet with the web hosting and web design, but quickly re-discovered his childhood love of video. Hope Farm, Inc. was instrumental in introducing him to the business of video; they wanted to have the ability to put videos on their website. "At the time," Crawford remembers, "they had photos and images, moving images and some scripts that allowed some jazzy things to happen on their site, which we don't use today, but they wanted to have some video as well. Back then, video wasn't exactly optimized, video hogged a lot of bandwidth. It wasn't the best time to utilize video for the site, but, it prompted me to start making recordings of different events and functions, promotional stuff for them. So that's how I got back in to video and fell in love with it again."

Crawford had dabbled in video when he was younger, going all the way back to his late teen years. "It was back in the days, with VCRs and Beta decks and just doing A/B cuts and things like that," he says. Over the years, Crawford has had the opportunity to utilize his video skills for high profile companies including New York Life where he created a series of training videos which were distributed to several different countries and translated into different languages, those videos were used for sales personnel throughout their organization. It was at that point, Crawford says that he realized his long term goal was to be an entrepreneur and provide a web-based video service for his customers.

Today, Crawford helps entrepreneurs and small businesses engage effectively to convert prospects into customers by using strategic marketing with an emphasis on video content, and social media. I've become well-versed in creating video that is impactful. I focus on creating truly valuable content and really understanding, listening, and communicating the message that the client wants to portray. I help them craft that message, shape it and mold it in a way that's going to produce the best result."

Crawford also teaches them how to leverage the video content they have using social media sites as a platform to increase brand awareness. Crawford has written a book, "Video Social Creative, Marketing With Video and Social Media To Convert Prospects Into Customers" which will be released in 2014 through Amazon and other online retailers.

Video is one of the most effective methods of positioning yourself as an authority. Audio content is great. Printed material definitely has its advantages. But video commands the attention of the viewer more than any other media and provides the single greatest opportunity for you to build rapport so that your prospects get to like, know, and trust you as the authority in your field.

"My family is the single most important reason why I am engaged in this entrepreneurial endeavor. Without my family, I would most likely not be doing this," Crawford explains, "I have a wife and three sons, which I'm very proud of. So thankful to celebrate my twentieth anniversary this year," he adds.

I serve in the media ministry in my church. For me, I feel that's the best use of my time and talent, to serve in that manner–to help impact someone else's life through what I know and what I have been gifted with.

For more information about Noble, visit: http://www.NobleCrawford.com.

To learn more about his digital marketing agency, Video Social Creative visit http://www.videosocialcreative.com.

ROGER DUE

BUSINESS: Manzano Software Company

EMAIL: rogerdue@gmail.com

LOCATION: Albuquerque, New Mexico

FACEBOOK: Facebook.com/roger.due

LINKEDIN: LinkedIn.com/in/rogerdue

SKYPE: roger.due

Roger Due grew up on an Indiana dairy farm as the eldest of 9 and was very active in 4H and science projects. In junior high, he helped sell snacks to people viewing the 4H cattle presentations at the county fairgrounds. In the Fall, he would sell Christmas cards. "My objective was to get off the farm," he explains, "I went to school to study Physics and my original idea was to get a PhD in Experimental Nuclear Physics. Instead I got my Bachelor's degree, and later I went back to school to get my MBA."

Due worked in the Boston area high tech industry until 1991.

He and his wife then moved to Albuquerque, New Mexico. "We first lived in a community-based, housing organization where there were about 95 condos. We had our own roads, water plant, sewer plant, and everything was self-governed. I got elected to the Board. I didn't quite realize what I was getting into, but I was on the Board for three years; the first year as Secretary and the next two years as Board President," Due says.

Due has an ability that a lot of people aren't willing to exercise. He was able to walk into dynamic situations with people of different temperaments and personalities and assess the situation and pull together a solution that would work for everyone. There was a situation with one of the tenants that had gone on for seven years. The Board was constantly sending him letters requesting specific actions and he kept ignoring them.

So Due said, "Well, I'll take a look at that." So he went up and talked with the owner who said, "You're the first person who's ever set foot in my home and talked with me about this situation." Due came to an agreement with him and got it solved. Due was also instrumental in getting a major revision of the Bylaws written and approved, and upgrading the sewer plant to extend its life for another 20 years.

Due is known as a troubleshooter and the Solutions Guy. When you want a workable solution, let him take a look at all the parts and he'll come up with something that a lot of folks may not have thought about. He's a problem solver. "It was a real wake up to realize that I had this skill of working with such a diverse group of community people to formulate and implement solutions in very challenging situations," Due says.

Today, Due specializes in an area of business websites called responsive design. Basically, that means that the website is built to contain all of the pieces needed for it to correctly display all content, regardless of the devices used to view it — whether it's an iPhone, a tablet, or a laptop. With this type of design the same content is dynamically rearranged and resized so that it will display correctly on all devices without having to zoom and scroll right/left.

"We know that over fifty percent of the searches these days are done on smartphones and mobile devices. Having a website that provides a great user experience across all devices translates into increased revenue for the business. For example, in the real estate industry, think of the home shopper. They're driving around town with their smartphone. Well, isn't it a good idea to be able to have easy access to the possible home information out there on your smartphone? If you want to have an exercise in frustration, try looking at a typical real estate website on your smartphone. You'll go crazy trying to find the information, since most of these websites were designed for desktop browsers and not the smartphones."

In addition to his technical background as a problem solver and trouble shooter, his wife is from the Black Forest area in Germany. She got him involved in a lot of outdoor activities. "I do a little bit of hiking with her," he says. "In 2009 we spent a whole month in Australia. We took our tent and camping gear with us and rented a car. We went from Melbourne to Adelaide to Ayers Rock to Alice Springs, camping the entire time, driving over 4,300 miles. We never stayed in a hotel once. Most of the time, we camped in the Outback. We made it a point to shop for our supplies where the locals would shop. We cooked our own food and were out in the Outback enjoying the wide open spaces and hiking with the locals. You get to see a much different side of people when you travel that way. The Australian's were very friendly."

"I have enough confidence in my abilities that I can work with a diverse group of people to find solutions for challenging requirements and get consensus for a successful implementation. As a manager, I never threatened by saying that you'd better do it my way or else. I always tried to bring people along and educate them as to the reasons we were doing things in a particular way when finding solutions. I think a lot of this ties in with how I've been able to solve a lot of the website problems that I've been working on in recent years. I take the time to understand the client's business, needs, and marketing objectives."

Visit LinkedIn for more information on Roger Due and ways to contact him:

http://www.LinkedIn.com/in/RogerDue

VALERIE DUVALL

BUSINESS: Pinpoint Digital

WEBSITE: PinpointDigitalSolutions.com

EMAIL: valerie@pinpointdigitalsolutions.com

LOCATION: Somers, NY

LINKEDIN: LinkedIn.com/in/valerieduvall1

Valerie DuVall, founder of New York based Pinpoint Digital, is certain she was born an entrepreneur. "As early as I can remember, I was always looking for ways to make money — whether it was a paper route or selling lemonade on the corner."

Like many successful business owners, she's taken on and excelled at different ventures in the search for that one magical opportunity that fuels the entrepreneur's spirit. She found that in Marketing and Advertising. And just like so many entrepreneurial success stories, it wasn't the target she had in her sights when she started out.

Discovering her passion and talent for helping local business owners and entrepreneurs build their customer base unfolded in front of her because she didn't wait for success to happen. She kept moving forward and opening news doors for herself.

Upon graduating high school, DuVall joined the military, worked hard and earned a scholarship from the Marine Corps to attend college.

After graduating with a BA in Economics from the University of Virginia, DuVall started her career as an intern with the bond market division of a large Wall Street firm. Her ability to see problems, create and execute successful solutions gained DuVall the honor of being the fastest person to rise through the ranks from Intern to Vice President within the firm.

Even though she was quickly gaining financial success, she realized there was something missing. She decided not to waste time doing something she didn't love.

DuVall made the decision to turn her back on the Wall Street paycheck to follow her passion for interior design and started Valerie DuVall Interiors. "I know it sounds kooky," she says, "Going from a Wall Street career to interior design, but I think I just wanted a hundred percent change in direction. How different can it be, I thought, going from the financial world to decorating houses?"

As any new business owner knows, generating leads and building a customer base is first priority if the doors are to remain open. She knew the Internet was the place she needed to be found.

By teaching herself how to get her design business online, DuVall discovered what would become a much deeper passion... the world of Internet Marketing.

"Looking for ideas online," she remembers, "I stumbled across a product that taught how to build a website. Back in those days, they didn't have WordPress. I don't even think it was html. It was a coding nightmare, but in the back of my mind, the Internet was there. The seed was planted, that the Internet would be a great way to connect with potential customers and build a business."

DuVall consumed and mastered everything she could about being found online. Blogging, SEO, Paid Traffic, all the things that the search engine gurus were talking about and business owners knew very little about. Valerie quickly found herself being referred to as an Internet Marketing Expert. Several nearby businesses began coming to her, not for interior design advice, but for Online Marketing consultations.

One thing that set DuVall apart from all the self proclaimed "Search Engine, Get On The Front Page of Google Experts" was that she understood that even though online traffic was important, it was really where the marketing part begins.

"SEO, paid traffic, guest blogging, guest podcasting: all these things are important. You need to get out there. You need traffic. But once people come to your website, that's when the magic happens. You need to be the one they choose. And to do that, you've got to show that you are an authority. You've got to be the one where they say, 'Yes, this is the person that can help me'," DuVall says.

This was her true passion, that one magic opportunity that fuels the entrepreneur's spirit. DuVall knew what she had to do and founded Pinpoint Digital in 2008. Since then, she has been helping local and national companies to "pinpoint" their perfect online strategy, and that goes way beyond SEO and just getting a website found online.

Pinpoint focuses on getting their clients new customers and increasing the ROI for current prospects and customers. DuVall says, "What I can offer to a company, entrepreneur or coach is my perspective. I look at a client's business from high above and find the holes. Whether the issue is SEO or promotion, if they're not getting traffic — in the end, it is all about being the one potential customers choose."

To learn more about Valerie DuVall visit her LinkedIn at: https://www.linkedin.com/pub/valerie-DuVall/11/858/6ab.

For more information about her company Pinpoint Digital visit: http://pinpointdigitalsolutions.com/.

ELOISE EDWARDS-GIRON

BUSINESS: Successful IM, LLC

LOCATION: Short Hills, New Jersey

FACEBOOK: Facebook.com/successfulimllc

TWITTER: Twitter.com/Successfulim1

EMAIL: eloisegiron@yahoo.com

"At a very early age," Eloise Edwards-Giron says, "I watched my mother work for very long hours each day. She was a seamstress, and she also baked for a living. That was her job, she was her own boss. My mother helped other people meet their needs and in return she got paid for her services. Since my dad was not actively involved, she was able to support her family and other children who were under her care with the proceeds from her business."

She adds, "Many days I would just imagine how different life would be if my mom could just spend some quality time with us, as so many of my friends' parents did. The irony was that my mother was very successful at what she did and was able to provide us with a very affluent lifestyle, including a higher education, whereas my friends´ parents, who spent quality time with them, but worked a 9 to 5 were barely able to take care of their family financially. Even the retired folks in the neighborhood were just scrambling to make ends meet." She thought, if she could just be as successful as her mother, yet be able to spend quality time with her family, it would be ideal.

Compassion and caring for others led her to pursue the nursing career, becoming a Registered Nurse. Since nursing was in high demand at the time, she felt that she would be able to help people as well as make good money. "I started my nursing career working for an institution, but my goal was to become an entrepreneur. Soon I discovered that the nursing career wasn't as lucrative as I thought, so now I started to do some overtime with the erroneous idea that 'more work equals more money'. I thought this would propel me into financial freedom which would eventually provide me with the finances needed to make my entrepreneurship dream a reality. It didn't work."

Next she sought numerous activities to make money such as selling vacuums, joining multi-level marketing type businesses until she was introduced to Internet Marketing. Edwards-Giron knew she was interested in entrepreneurship and that Internet Marketing was for her when she made her very first online profit. It was through the currency trading (The Forex Market). With no previous experience on how it worked, she was instructed by one of the online employees of this company that all she needed to know was to: "Buy when the currency (Dollar) or (Euro) was low, and sell when it was high." That was exactly what she did. "On the seventh day of trading in this currency market I noticed a profit of $3,000," she says. "I was blown away. It felt great, now I was more determined to make more money online, but I also knew the risk of losing what I had made."

In 2009, Edwards-Giron started to listen to finance radio stations in order to become educated about investing money. At the time, the talk was about the prediction of the increase value of silver and gold within the next five years. This sounded like a great opportunity to Edwards-Giron, so she decided to put currency trading on pause and took her $3,000 and reinvested it into the gold market, only that this time a broker was assigned to her.

Three weeks later, she received a call from her broker with the news that her investment had a drastic increase of $18,000. After his commission, she made a profit of $15,000. "I could not believe it, I was flabbergasted!" she says. "My broker reminded me that this was not a typical outcome, and that I had made a 'home run.' He also reinforced the risk there is in trading," she adds.

"Now, the fact that I was able to make that kind of money, in such short time with both type of trading really got me on 'a hype' for a few days." She enjoyed the fact that now knew a way of making cash without hard labor. "I felt like money was just knocking at my door. Nonetheless, deep within me there was a sense of discomfort due to the uncertainty of these markets. This experience felt like 'self-gratification,' 'like a gamble,' and there was 'so much uncertainty'. I'm sure there are people who make a good living from this, but I did not know all the matrices, so I left it alone."

Later on Edwards-Giron decided to surf the Internet and

came across "Now I truly felt the assurance that I can become the business person I dreamt of," she says.

Last November, Edwards-Giron was able to create a mobile site for a small gift shop. "I got $500 for the setup fee and $50 for maintenance fee," Edwards-Giron says, "The owner of this shop gave me five referrals of which, two of them got a mobile site, and the other three said they are interested in a regular site. At last this feels like a real business. I was able to help someone with their business, and get proceeds from it in return."

As she took a closer look at the Internet Marketing industry, she realized that there are lots of businesses affected by deterring statements being made about them, some of which they were not even aware of, this lead to her starting to offer a new service in her business. She reaches out to these business owners and offers help in repairing not just their reputation, but their online presence. Edwards-Giron's business also offers Reputation Marketing to small and medium size businesses.

"I position myself as the educator and advocate for all my prospects. I help them create a positive online presence by building an outstanding reputation, so they can attract new customers and retain existing ones," she explains. "I put my prospects first. It's all about helping business owners achieve their goal. Once I complete one task, I look for another one that will even improve their business; as a result they are able to get a higher return on their investment."

To learn more about Eloise Edwards-Giron visit her LinkedIn at:
https://www.LinkedIn.com/profile/view?id=68421253.

T. ALLEN HANES

BUSINESS:	T. Allen Hanes & Associates
WEBSITE:	TheAuthoritySyndicate.com
EMAIL:	tracyahanes@gmail.com
LOCATION:	Houston, Texas
FACEBOOK:	Facebook.com/tracy.hanes1
LINKEDIN:	https://www.linkedin.com/in/Tallenhanes
PHONE:	281-910-8728

T. Allen Hanes' entry point into entrepreneurialism was at an early age. One of the first experiences he had as an entrepreneur was when every year in Indianapolis, Indiana at a local radio station; they would have a raft race down the White River. He wanted to build a raft, but he didn't have any money to do it. The guy that owned the local grocery store was a big shot businessman and Hanes had always admired him.

Hanes explains, "I walked in there and introduced myself and said, 'Hey, I'd like to enter this raft race and I'm wondering if you're willing to fund it?' He said, 'Well, what's in it for me?' I said, 'I tell you what, I'll put your sign on my raft if you give me 50 bucks and we'll get you some marketing as we go down the river. He handed me $50 and I was hooked.' I thought, 'Man, that's pretty cool!' I guess I was 13 years old and that was my first local marketing deal that I ever did in my life."

From there Hanes had a love for photography. He would watch his father take pictures. He started studying photography books and modeled his pictures after well-known photographers. He took that and connected entrepreneurialism and he made a decision early on that he was going to be a photographer.

Hanes still has his first business card. It was called "Good Image Photography" and he secured a gig photographing a wealthy gentleman's inventory of his home for insurance purposes. He paid Hanes $500 to do that. "I was always envisioning myself running a business. I always had that vision from a young age. I'm not sure where it came from because my parents were hardworking blue-collar Americans, and worked hard at providing for me."

Hanes dropped out of college and he heard about being a photographer in the US Navy. He thought it would be a great idea to be able to travel the world, get paid for it, and do photography. Find your passion, he advises. Do what you love and love what you do. Ask yourself, What would I do even if I wasn't paid to do it?

Hanes retired as a US Navy Photographer and Video

Cameraman/Producer in 1998.

After retirement, "I had a couple of people approach me to form a company to consult on safety leadership. I used my leadership, Internet skills, video marketing, and positioning to position it in the market as the authority on this particular topic. It took off."

During that time, he says, one of his partners was an inventor. He knew nothing about publishing a book and he asked if Hanes knew anything about self-publishing. Hanes said, "No, but I'm willing to find out." That was in 2010.

Hanes explains, "I immersed myself on how to self-publish. I published this gentleman's first book and when I did he was so excited that I accomplished this for him. I mean, handing him that book was priceless. His face and his excitement were priceless and I was hooked. I knew that this was what I was supposed to do, solve that problem." Now, Hanes positions people in the marketplace as the authority by publishing their books, producing their podcasts, producing hangouts, and getting those footprints on the Internet so they can be found as the authority in their industry.

He's been married 25 years and met his wife in the Philippines when he was in the Navy. Hanes also has daughter who is just turning 20 and a son who is 24. His hobbies include golf, automobile racing, football, photography, video, and telling people's stories in book form.

For more information about T. Allen Hanes visit his LinkedIn at: https://www.linkedin.com/in/Tallenhanes

ELIZABETH HARTENBERGER

BUSINESS: Western Winds Management Consulting Inc.

WEBSITE: AuthorityMarketingMatters.com

EMAIL: Elizabeth@AuthorityMarketingMatters.com

LOCATION: Toronto, Ontario CANADA

FACEBOOK: Facebook.com/elizabeth.hartenberger.7

When potential prospects and customers are ready to buy, Elizabeth Hartenberger, a Marketing Consultant and Online Media Strategist, enables them to not only **find** you and your business, but to **choose** your business. She then helps turn these customers into your loyal raving fans.

"As a service professional, consultant or local small business, your reputation *is* your brand," Hartenberger says. "We help you build and leverage a 5-star reputation for your firm. And then we help establish you, the business or practice owner, as the expert and authority in your field."

"Your customers become your loyal and raving fans when they realize that you care about them, you educate them, and you become an advocate for their success," she adds.

In her 30+ years in corporate life at IBM, Ms. Hartenberger became a collaborative and trusted advisor for all her clients. She applies these same techniques in her work with you and your business.

Elizabeth Hartenberger grew up on the prairies in a small town of ten thousand people where virtually everyone was an entrepreneur. "We didn't realize that was something special, you know? Everyone ran their own business," she says. She started out doing entrepreneurial things like most kids do—shoveling snow in the winter time, and babysitting from the age of twelve. Earning her first real money was exciting and kept her motivated to do more.

By grade nine, Hartenberger became an Avon sales representative. "Back then it was door-to-door sales of cosmetics and toiletries," she says, "Remember – 'Ding dong! Avon calling'. It was fun and I was very, very successful at it, actually. I became the youngest top-selling rep in my entire territory, having achieved some phenomenal sales. I even won major awards for it."

Hartenberger still remembers that initial excitement. "I had money for the first time that was fairly substantial. I met a lot of people. Right from the start, I was a mentor to people. I taught my customers how to look and feel gorgeous with the products they bought from me. I liked to help people become the best they could be and I've continued that philosophy all the way throughout my business life."

"I grew up in a small town, so when I went to 'the big city' for University, I was really intrigued by the mystique of the corporate business world," she explains. When she graduated, Elizabeth came to Toronto and worked for IBM, a Fortune 100 company. Hartenberger finished her MBA at the same time. "There was no such thing as an Executive MBA then. So many CEOs and COOs were students, right alongside me."

What Hartenberger found really fascinating was that the C-suite Executives who shared her classes were not the 'God of Gods'. "They, like everyone else," she says, "put their pants on one leg at a time. It made me realize that even though they were recognized experts in their field, they were still just people, and that helped a lot as I moved forward with my own business."

Ms. Hartenberger worked as an Executive Project Manager in IBM's Professional Services Division throughout her corporate career before starting her own business.

"People who knew me always laughed, because I kept saying, 'Oh, I'm going to be leaving in two years. I'm going to start my own business and work for myself.' And I said that every year for the entire 30+ years that I worked in the corporate world. But every year or two I'd start a new project gig, and it felt like I *was* running my own business."

In her role as a Project Manager, Hartenberger used many entrepreneurial skills. "I was considered the expert troubled project firefighter, meaning that I went around the world working on projects. If a project was anywhere from $50 million to $100 million dollars over budget and three to five years behind schedule, I would bring a team in. We'd work four to eight months, sometimes longer, to help put the project back on its track. Stabilize it so that it could either be shut down cleanly, or finish through to completion, successfully and effectively," she explains.

Hartenberger remembers her big retirement plan, "I was going to retire on a Friday and on a Monday start working on a new gig with a new client, doing the same management consulting work that I did before, but for myself." She adds, "I also wanted to continue doing travel writing and travel photography on the side. The travel writing was where I thought I was really going to make the bulk of my entrepreneurial income, and live 'the writers life'."

In 2011, Ms. Hartenberger left the constraints of corporate life. In addition to marketing consulting, she began copywriting from a B2B perspective (business-to-business), working for clients in the software, technology and Professional Services industries. Mid-way through 2012, she joined up with Information Marketer, Dan Kennedy, to provide copywriting and consulting for Infomarketers*. (Dan is famous globally as being one of the top marketers and supporting information marketers in developing their business.)

These days, she works with local businesses nationwide and internationally, focusing on creating and building the reputation of the business and then positioning the business or practice owner as an authority and an expert in their field. Hartenberger uses a variety of strategies to achieve this, including hosting Google Hangout interviews, publishing client's articles and books, and creating video testimonials. She gets clients featured on podcasts, uses press releases to get media attention and then markets the business reputation to prospective clients online.

"If you think about it," she says, "If you've got a business or practice owner that's also shown to have some expert positioning and credibility, then that gives a lot of credence to people actually choosing you, picking *your* business. If all else is equal, who are they going to pick? They're going to pick someone that's got multiple five-star reviews, and a business or a practice owner that's a recognized authority in their field."

"I like to add value. I believe that every encounter that I have, every engagement that I have with a client, I want to leave them with much more than what they started with," Hartenberger explains. "I lead with value. I end with value. I deliver results. I like to get paid based on performance."

Elizabeth has published several Special Reports about the power of Case Studies to demonstrate a customer testimonial, and the art of Story Telling to create these Case Studies. She is also currently working on a family project, to publish and share her Grandma's handwritten recipes from the early years of her Marriage, vintage 1921.

In her free time, Hartenberger volunteers at blues music festivals and events; she's an avid lover of blues music and a member of her local Toronto Blues Society. She also loves to travel. "I've had the honour and privilege of living and working in many cities and countries around the globe, as well as travelling for personal fun and adventure. I consider myself a citizen of the world." She is a member of her Condo Board of Directors, and lives with Alex, her 19-year old ferocious feline.

To learn more about Elizabeth Hartenberger please visit her LinkedIn page at: http://ca.linkedin.com/in/elizabethhartenberger.

The Dan Kennedy Copywriter for Info-Marketers Certification is awarded to professional copywriters who have successfully completed a course of study of preparation for such copywriting.

BRIAN HORN

FACEBOOK: Facebook.com/brian.horn

Brian Horn is long time entrepreneur and writer for The Huffington Post on the topic of "authority marketing".

He is also a 3 time best selling author that has helped many top celebrity entrepreneurs with their online branding and marketing.

Brian consulted exclusively with these celebrity entrepreneurs for nearly 5 years before exploding onto the scene in 2009. He has since has been profiled and featured on Wall Street Journal, ABC, NBC, CBS, Fox, Forbes, Advertising Age and dozens of other media outlets.

In 2010, Inc Magazine named an "emerging business leader to watch."

Brian's goal is to find the magic in each of his clients, help them position it, get national media attention for it, and leverage that attention into more customers and profits.

He is also an in demand speaker that has traveled the world entertaining and educating audiences.

ART KOSTER

BUSINESS: www.ArtKoster.com

WEBSITE: ArtKoster.com

EMAIL: Media@ArtKoster.com

LOCATION: Columbus, Ohio

FACEBOOK: Facebook.com/arthur.koster.5

Art Koster is a Best Selling Author, Media Strategist, and Founder of AuthorityNewsMedia.com and ArtKoster.com, a results-driven reputation marketing and Authority PR agency. He is a non-techie marketing machine with celebrity savvy, a sucker for children's charities and an obsession for client authority branding.

Every author who works with Art enjoys the magic of becoming a Best Selling Author and a newly recognized authority in the media. Art has been featured on ABC, NBC, CBS, FOX, Wall Street Journal, Worth Magazine, CNN, and dozens of news publications such as The Boston Globe.

William James once said, "Success or failure depends more upon attitude than upon capacity. Successful men act as though they have accomplished or are enjoying something. Soon it becomes a reality. Act, look, feel successful, conduct yourself accordingly, and you will be amazed at the positive results."

Entrepreneur Art Koster puts these principles to work every day, believing in the use of positive attitude and strong work ethic to accomplish big things and find success in his own business by helping others reach their own goals and dreams.

"People gravitate towards authorities. They can't help it. That person has got 'it'," Koster says. Art Koster started AuthorityNewsMedia.com in 2014 and turned his focus to helping people become recognized authorities in their field because having that media exposure helps businesses find that "it" factor.

"I've been able to help people do things they never thought they had the ability or opportunity to accomplish before. I get to feel the same joy my clients get when they outshine their competition, feeling the genuine appreciation that comes pouring in from their influence circle towards them. And let's not kid ourselves, my clients enjoy the jump in their income as well that comes with being a trusted authority like Dan Kennedy and Dave Ramsey," Koster says.

Koster was pulled into entrepreneurialism inadvertently when his family started their own business during his college years.

"I was the first in my family to attend college. I received a full academic scholarship to one of the top ranked business universities by U.S. News & World Report in the Midwest, John Carroll University. However, when my family purchased a ServPro franchise, I was pulled into working for them in the summers. Instead of interning at local corporations, I was down in basements pulling up some nasty, nasty things that people once claimed was carpet," Koster explains, "metaphorically, it was spot on for corporate life."

As grads were and are supposed to do, Koster graduated from college and tried the corporate world. "I spent a year with MBNA," he says, "After a year of watching some of the legal but questionable business practices and seeing how my salary was tied to meeting quotas that weren't in the best interest of their clients, I couldn't continue to do it. I knew I needed to do something different." I went to California for a bit, then came back to Cleveland, Ohio and helped expand the family business with a second ServPro franchise. After getting it up and running, I eventually sold my share and I went into the mortgage industry which was booming at the time."

"The first time I really considered myself an entrepreneur was when I pulled in what seemed like a ridiculous amount in one month at the time with my first call team I pieced together," Koster says. "I couldn't sell a lick myself, but I was great at coordinating teams."

He opened his own branch in Myrtle Beach investigating the vacation property market and enjoying the beach, but found he missed city amenities and the larger pool of nearby destinations for quick vacation escapes, and so moved back to Columbus. By then the housing market bubble had burst, and it was time for a new venture.

"At that time, I think I just typed in what everyone probably does when they first think about working in an online business: 'Make money online'," he says.

Until 2009 Koster didn't see himself as a marketer, even though he was doing affiliate marketing at the time. Marketing Expert, Jack Mize, introduced him to authority marketing and to seeing himself as both an educator and an advocate for businesses. From then on, he shifted his focus to using local marketing to help people.

Koster tells up-and-coming entrepreneurs and marketers, "Being an entrepreneur is not easy. Taking off and getting it started is not easy. It takes perseverance in continuing to try and making mistakes. Sometimes it means not listening when people say something is not possible.

But, you know, if you keep going, keep learning, you connect with the right people. You find the right things and if you really want something, you can make it happen. There've been times that I've lost everything. I had and I always will tell myself that if I can do it once, I can do it again. It goes back to that old saying of it's how many times you get up, not how many times you fall."

He adds, "Believe in the possibilities. Be the educator. You are the expert. Believe that tomorrow can be even better than today. And here's the big one: believe in yourself."

Koster enjoys spending time consistently educating himself, having BBQ's, then working off the BBQ's, and spending time with his family. He is also a self-noted fan who enjoys his weekends during the Fall watching Ohio State and Cleveland Browns' football, when every Saturday he's enjoying a little Columbus style Mardi Gras.

VICTOR LITTLE

LOCATION: Pakenham, Victoria

WEBSITE: Marketingezi.com

FACEBOOK: Facebook.com/victor.little.357

LINKED IN: LinkedIn.com/pub/victor-little/7/860/823

TWITTER: Twitter.com/victorjlittle

Victor Little first started selling services to his neighbors at six or seven years old. He lived in a small town in Australia called Somerville. "My friends and I, we decided that we needed some pocket money. So we used to go around to houses and ask if they had any jobs to do. And what we found was a couple of them used to feel sorry for us and give us money, even though we didn't do any work."

Later on, when Little was about ten, he moved to a town called Cheltenham and started a lawn mowing business with his father. "I had an old lawn mower that I used to have to start by electric motor and then run it around to where I was mowing and come back, and making sure that I didn't stop the lawn mower," he remembers. Little and his dad also collected junk to sell or trade. "When we had junk heap days, when everyone puts junk out in the front, we used to go around and collect steel, bottles, anything we could trade or sell." At fourteen he started a chemist round service, where he would deliver chemist parcels to people all around the town six days a week. At fifteen, Little started a little handyman business, going around to people's houses and fixing things.

As a teen he tried out several different businesses. "I did some engineering work, I used to build trampolines and I used to make some car components. It brought in about a hundred dollars a week. That was actually quite a bit of money and I bought my first stereo," Little remembers.

"When I was almost sixteen," Little says, "My dad had just died so I decided I'd become an apprentice. So I took up a four year apprenticeship when I was sixteen. Even with an apprenticeship, I got a second job after work. In the meantime, I was also buying and fixing and selling machines."

After finishing his apprenticeship, Little started an engineering job. After a few months, he got promoted to Foreman and shortly thereafter, to Manager. "Karl, the owner, and myself, took the company from a three-man operation into about twenty-eight people over a period of less than ten years turning over millions of dollars in business," Little explains.

"In 1990, I went overseas for about six months, when I came back, Karl's business was gone in those six months. I left in

February 1990 and we were the busiest we'd ever been. I came back six months later and it was all over." It was then that Little decided to become an entrepreneur and start his own business.

"I realized that I wanted to be in charge of my own destiny," Little says, "Therefore I needed my own product. I wanted to be in manufacturing, but I just wanted my own product, because I had discovered, that if you don't have your own product, you're not in control. What I was looking for was a product that I could manufacture. I was looking for a business that had gone broke or some products that I could buy cheaply as I had no money. I had less than a thousand dollars when I came back from overseas... in the end, I started my scrap metal business and worked away, and I turned over $10,000 in my first year. The next year, I turned over $110,000 and I had $10,000 cash in my hand at any particular stage. So it ended up being quite good."

As his success rose, people began to bring Little business and investment opportunities. "I ended up purchasing a company called Deps," Little explains, "It's been running for twenty-five years now. It's a specialized pipe manufacturing business that makes bore casing and screens for drilling, mining and civil engineering, also we manufacture bore pumps, especially for farming irrigation. We took this from a $200K in the first year, to over $2 million worth of sales."

After attending the Internet Marketing Summit Little learned about the power of Internet Marketing to help businesses. One of the companies Little now runs is marketingezi.com. The bottom line of marketingeze.com is to help clients to get more customers, stand out and be seen as an expert in their field.

"I've now been running businesses for well over twenty-five years on my own, owning them, plus I've been running businesses, for more than thirty years. And the last ten years I've been learning about marketing. In this time, there are two major learnings that I have discovered," Little says, "One is my 'why'."

"My 'why' is to be a leader and inspire others to compete with change while having fun. The second part is 'who am I'. I am integrity and passion and that is who I am. So with these two, I realize I must help you succeed where possible."

KURT LUCIEN

BUSINESS: Karitsu, Inc.

WEBSITE: HowDoYouGetMoreCustomers.com

EMAIL: info@KurtLucien.com

LOCATION: NewYork, New York

PHONE: 1-646-543-6532

LINKEDIN: LinkedIn.com/in/kurtlucien/

FACEBOOK: Facebook.com/TheSuccessDirector

Kurt Lucien is a Best Selling Author, Business Growth and Marketing Director, as well as the Founder HowDoYouGetMoreCustomers.com, a Reputation and Influence Marketing Agency. "I come from an entrepreneurial family linage," Kurt Lucien explains, "For as far back as I can trace — on both sides of my family — they were self-employed as shop owners, carpenters, building & remodeling contractors, seamstresses, cake makers, event planners, and farmers. With that being my foundation, it's no surprise that I would barter with my grandmother who was my guardian, as well as an expert seamstress and cake maker. Those earliest forms of bartering services, where I would negotiate my payment for assisting with her many projects gave me the values and understanding of what being an entrepreneur means.'

As an adult, Lucien's passion for technology lead him to obtaining a Master's degree in Technology Management while being the Information Technology Operations Manager for one of the top five advertising companies worldwide.

His switch to Online Marketing happened in 2005 when a company downsize left him looking to follow his true passion: helping others succeed.

Lucien learned everything he could about Online Marketing before starting his new entrepreneurial venture. He even became a certified Life, Health and Business coach. He spent countless hours learning about a variety of Online Marketing techniques such as Referral Marketing, List Building, Reputation Marketing, Search Engine Optimization (SEO), Social Media Management, Mobile Marketing, WordPress development and optimization for Mobile Applications.

"To 'cut my teeth' as they would say, into this new industry," Lucien says, "I offered my services to help friends and family members; as well as, the local small businesses I frequented. I offered to help them get more customers for their business. It was when I heard and saw the success our joint efforts created — I was sold, I knew without a doubt, that this is what I'm supposed to be doing at this point in my life. This is what all my years of learning, trials, errors and successes have prepared me for — helping those with an entrepreneurial spirit and drive succeed!

Today with the ever changing and evolving online world, having a knowledgeable, trusted, reliable; some would even say, expert marketing consultant managing a company's (brand) online visibility is a necessity in this day and age.

Today, Lucien helps entrepreneurs, professionals, small businesses and even corporations increase their online visibility; get more traffic by engagement which generates leads, that convert to customers, resulting in positive revenue, profits, and return on investments.

"I help their brand become a celebrity within their industry, then market that newly achieved status to get more exposure, more traffic and more ROI from their marketing investment," Lucien adds. Lucien's online marketing strategies are geared toward transforming leads into customers — not just any customer, but the kind of loyal customers who will be inclined to spread the good word.

In his free time, Kurt Lucien loves traveling, dancing and learning (the subject doesn't matter). He loves learning about people, cultures, new activities and having new experiences. He believes in living life to its fullest and embraces the motto, "I'm here — I'm present!"

To learn more about Kurt Lucien visit: http://kurtlucien.com.

For more information about his company Karitsu, Inc. visit: http://howdoyougetmorecustomers.com

STEPHANIE MILLER

BUSINESS: PRO-FOUND

WEBSITE: ProfoundProcess.com

EMAIL: info@profoundprocess.com

LOCATION: Downeast, Maine

FACEBOOK: Facebook.com/profoundprocess

LINKEDIN: LinkedIn.com/pub/stephanie-
              miller/4/a28/5a9/

TWITTER: Twitter.com/profoundprocess

Stephanie Miller fell in love with business and entrepreneurship in grade school. Back then, she charged the kids in the neighborhood five cents for art lessons. She says, "It combined my love of art with teaching. I still have the first award I ever won back in Junior High from an ad design contest run by the local newspaper. The client was a community bank. Seeing my work in print sparked an eternal flame."

Miller went on to manage a party goods store where she became "a marketing junkie." She got started when she introduced costume rentals to the mix of products and designed her first Val-Pak ad to promote it.

"I'll never forget the day after the coupons hit, she says, "The parking lot filled with customers who lined up out the door to rent costumes. We had record sales. From that point on, I focused on creating a buzz, making the phone ring and attracting customers."

Miller co-founded a successful equipment finance company in the Boston area back in 1995. She was responsible for everything from HR and bookkeeping to sales and marketing. While she enjoyed working with business owners nationwide, she craved the challenge of starting a new venture on her own, outside corporate environs.

She moved to Maine, sold her interest in the business and started a new business called PRO-FOUND. Within a year, she met her future husband. During this time, she designed a website to help sell her home and surprisingly, it sold within three months at the start of the worst economy.

Then she designed another website that helped sell a farm property she and her husband owned. When a friend mentioned they had been trying to sell a farmhouse for years with no luck, Miller offered to design a website. When her friend's farm sold, word got out that she had a knack for designing websites that resulted in sales. These days, the web design aspect of Miller's business is all by word-of-mouth referrals. Her clients include homeowners and business owners.

Miller's motto has always been, "Just Do It!" so she never had a crossover point from wanting to be an entrepreneur/ marketer to being one. She just did it. "I'm proud to offer unique, affordable community-based marketing that is news-worthy and helps everyone from local businesses to Non-profit organizations to the members of a community," she says.

Through her business, Miller shares what it takes to become an expert in the art of promotion, discovery and recovery. "I do this by implementing 'The PRO-FOUND Process,' a customized marketing plan that provides local and national exposure, recognition as a community partner and expert status in your industry."

She adds, "I understand marketing is an art form that uses skills, techniques and experience to get results. The mechanics of marketing — the media relations, writing and direct mail used to position you as the authority in your industry is my expertise; however they are not the artistry. I help you never waste money on advertising again.

I discovered the magic of how it is done first-hand, and have personally experienced the rewards of community marketing, being featured in the media and being recognized as an authority in my industry. When you search for a marketer to partner with, you don't look for an ordinary mechanic, you want to look for an artist."

Miller is a Cape Ann native, now living and working in coastal Maine with her husband, three cats and a dog. When she's not working with clients, she can either be found kayaking, tending the vegetable and woodland gardens or creating chaos in the kitchen.

JACK MIZE

WEBSITE: InfluencersRadio.com

FACEBOOK: Facebook.com/jackmize

LINKEDIN: LinkedIn.com/in/jackmize

Influencers Radio Host and Online Media Strategist Jack Mize is laser focused on helping entrepreneurs and professionals position themselves as educators and advocates for the success of their clients and prospects.

In addition to consulting directly with leaders in the fields of business, finance, health, real estate and personal development, Mize has helped hundreds of marketing consultants and media agencies grow their businesses with his outside the box strategies to boost client authority and positioning within their industry.

His philosophy was born out of what at first seemed to be a major conflict with no obvious solution. Mize realized very early that a career in sales was far more profitable than a fixed paycheck. But he discovered one big problem... he couldn't stand traditional selling. "I hate selling, but I love making people want to buy," Mize proclaims. There had to be a way to reconcile this contradiction, he thought.

"Getting paid for results rather than activity always drove me to work smarter and harder," he says. "Sales was the clear path, but I had to do it my way."

Jobs such as selling newspaper and cable television subscriptions door to door were always available, mainly because they were commission only and they had a revolving door of applicants that would be filtered out quickly by rejection and failure with little to no pay. Even so, for Mize it was to be the quickest option for a young entrepreneur in the making to earn bigger paychecks while working fewer hours than his friends flipping burgers for minimum wage.

Income was unpredictable, and there were even some slumps where he'd find himself with nothing to show for a week of hitting the pavement, knocking on doors. It was the rejection he hated, the feeling he was trying to talk someone into something for his benefit, not theirs.

Once he figured out that knocking on the door and quickly unloading a round of "Do you want to buy.... " before he heard the dreaded "not today" or "we can't afford it right now" was not doing the trick. That's when he came up with his "Don't sell – Make them want to buy" strategy.

It was all in the positioning and the results were remarkable.

One of the things the Cable Company "asked" salespeople to do, for no additional pay, was to make a note of which houses on each street had dogs in the backyard because their installers would need access to cable boxes.

Mize took this opportunity to reposition himself from a cable salesman to an "auditor" for the cable company. "I would simply knock on doors and introduce myself as an auditor for the cable company and let them know that we were going to be doing some work on their street over the next week and needed to know if they kept any dogs in the backyard. People that didn't have cable would always reply with 'but we don't have cable' and I would explain that the main wires ran thorough everyone's backyard and we may need access to theirs."

This removed one of the biggest things Mize hated about selling door to door, which was launching into a pitch as soon as they opened the door.

Once the resident understood why he was asking they would give him the information. He would thank them and just as he would turn to leave he would pivot back and say "By the way, they wanted me to let you know that since they are going to be out here anyway that they are waiving installation charges if you wanted to start getting all the channels and movies hooked up next week."

With that repositioning, Mize never felt the same kind of rejection because he got to present the special deal, not as a salesman, but as someone passing along valuable information. Sure he'd get plenty of "No thanks," but the warmest prospects, and there were plenty, would ask him to tell them more.

Mize no longer felt that he was trying to talk them into

something just for his benefit, it was for theirs, helping them choose options and explain why they shouldn't get certain channels because they were just repeats of another channel they were already getting.

He didn't have to sell. They wanted to buy and he was able to help them with their decisions. They looked at him as an authority, an educator and advocate. Some would even call their neighbors and let them in on this "inside deal" and they would have their doors open and ready to subscribe.

The power of this positioning earned Mize top "salesperson" for many months, even though he never felt like he had to sell.

As an Online Media Strategist, Mize has adjusted and tuned his strategies over the years. By helping his clients reposition themselves from traditional hard sales tactics to being the Educators and Advocates for their prospects and customers success, Jack has been credited with saving businesses and changing lives.

JAMES MOUX, MBA

LINKEDIN: LinkedIn.com/pub/james-moux-
mba-crp/2/2b9/790

FACEBOOK: Facebook.com/james.moux

LOCATION: Middletown, Delaware

Thinking back, James Moux, started showing a talent for entrepreneurship when he was twelve, while delivering newspapers. He remembers, "When I was a paper boy, I was trying to find ways to expand my route and find new clients. I was always looking for ways to sell more subscriptions, so I could make more money."

Moux has worked in several different fields over the course of his career, gaining skills that he uses in his businesses today. In addition to his early experiences as a paper boy, and starting a magazine, he's also worked in the pharmaceutical industry in sales and later on, in marketing.

Moux then moved into real estate, specializing in residential real estate sales and mortgage financing. "And that's actually my main area of expertise: real estate marketing, from a real estate company standpoint. We market to get new clients, direct to consumers," Moux explains. "I work on lead generation for the business. I work with people who are looking to sell their current home, and also those looking to purchase and finance a new home," he adds.

Over the years Moux has been learning what he needs to know to be successful in business.

"It's been a steady process. Mostly I've been reading, taking courses and learning on my own," he says.

Moux is also a big fan of learning from others both in person and through online courses.

"I learned things in courses that I was able to apply to my real estate business that made a real difference," he explains. "As a real estate agent or broker you need to generate your own business. Many companies don't provide you with customer leads, so you have to be an entrepreneurial marketer to generate your own business. My preferred methods are online marketing, print and direct mail," he explains.

Moux adds "Since English is not my first language I wasn't always confident when it comes to cold calling and talking to people or even calling people over the phone. Taking courses and listening to podcasts and webinars has helped me improve my skills. I also thrive on learning from others in a group setting where people share what they've been doing. I belong to several mastermind groups where people freely share their successes and challenges. I figured, 'If they can do it, I can as well' and therefore I can help others be successful."

Moux is married to Dr. Shirley R. Moux, and has an 18-year-old son that works as a carpenter and a daughter who is nine. She's in elementary school and is a gymnast.

He has a Master of Business Administration from the University of Delaware. Moux enjoys watching MMA and boxing matches. He also loves to read and considers himself a lifelong marketing student.

"I don't think I'll ever know enough so I'm always looking to increase my knowledge," he says.

James Moux can be reached at:
https://www.LinkedIn.com/pub/james-moux-mba-crp/2/2b9/790

DIANA M. NEEDHAM

BUSINESS: Needham Business Consulting

WEBSITE: DianaMNeedham.com

EMAIL: Diana@DianaMNeedham.com

LOCATION: Chapel Hill, North Carolina

FACEBOOK: Facebook.com/diana.needham

LINKEDIN: LinkedIn.com/in/dianamneedham

TWITTER: Twitter.com/DianaMNeedham

Marketing Strategist and Online Media Strategist, Diana M. Needham, started Needham Business Consulting in 2008 following a 26 year term in the corporate world as Director and Vice President at JP Morgan Chase.

During those years Diana honed her leadership, communication, and business skills by refining banking processes and systems for performance and leading strategy teams. Now she has taken her experience to the street, focusing on sharing simple marketing systems for business growth to entrepreneurs and small business owners and serving as an advocate for their success.

Diana began her career in the banking industry. She rose from an entry level, hourly research clerk in 1981, to the Vice President and the Director of the Program Office of the Retail Bank, headquartered in Columbus, Ohio. For Diana, rising through the ranks of the corporate world was all about process orientation, being able to take the big picture and break it down into sequential, step-by-step activities that would lead to the ultimate goal, and doing her 'best work' while mentoring her staff and project teams.

When her bank was acquired by Chase in 2004, Diana accepted a highly visible leadership role. Managing transition teams to effectively integrate people, processes, and systems from both high-powered organizations, Diana began to notice that what she enjoyed most about her banking career -- the 'mentoring' of her staff and teams -- was becoming quickly a thing of the past. The constant pressure to "do more with less" simply did not allow time to invest in our greatest resource, which is people.

Soon realizing that without the ability to work closely with her staff and teams, all that was left were the processes, the long hours, the anxiety, and the paycheck. The position that served her well and for which she had been grateful, had changed enough to have her walk away from the corporate world, and into the entrepreneurial world.

Similar to the refinement of banking processes, Diana now leverages her planning, communication, and implementation skills, working closely with clients to streamline their businesses, step by step, and is again in a position of mentor and advocate for success.

She now works with entrepreneurs and small business owners to map out what Diana calls their 'fastest (simplest) path to cash.' I'm always planning marketing strategies from the perspective of asking: What is the fastest way for my clients to get in front of their ideal clients and to grow their visibility and expert status?"

Diana explains, "What I have discovered by working with hundreds of entrepreneurs and small business owners is that we tend to make things more complicated than they need to be. I am all about *keeping it simple* to take action, actually implement, and get real results (more profits, more income, and more clients). I help entrepreneurs and small business owners who are frustrated, overwhelmed, and stressed, to determine *how* to market their businesses and map out their 'fastest path to cash.' Being highly visible to their market is a critical key to success."

Diana is mother of two adult children and has two grand dogs and two grand cats. She loves fitness, yoga, meditation, personal development, and hanging out with entrepreneurial friends on Facebook and LinkedIn.

For more information and to connect with Diana Needham on LinkedIn visit: www.LinkedIn.com/in/dianamneedham/.

Learn more about Needham Business Consulting at: http://dianamneedham.com/.

BRIAN RICHARDS

BUSINESS: PetBiz Profits

WEBSITE: PetBizProfits.com

EMAIL: BrianR@PetBizProfits.com

LOCATION: Brisbane, Queensland, Australia

FACEBOOK: Facebook.com/briantrichards

Thirty-five years ago, Australian Brian Richards graduated from University with his Electrical Engineering degree and a Bachelor of Science in Computer Science. He went to work for the second largest computer company in the world marketing computer systems and writing software programs as well.

"As I got more into the sales side of things and got to understand my own sales process better as a Sales Engineer, my interest in computers changed dramatically," Richards says. "I was working seven days a week and writing software at night and on the weekends. Then I grew more interested in the actual businesses of my clients. I wanted to understand what they were trying to achieve in their businesses and how they were doing it. I was curious about their sales funnels and their whole marketing process."

"After six or seven years of such intensive computer work, I was becoming jaded with computers, to be honest," explains Richards, "I moved into self-employment at twenty-five, establishing a financial planning practice." Most financial planners were self-employed at that time. "Once I became self-employed, I grew even more interested in marketing," Richards remembers, "I learned quickly that if you don't bring the business in, then you starve. I soon got married and there was a lot of pressure on me as a young man to not just learn the ropes of financial planning, but to develop a consistent marketing funnel."

One breakthrough Richards had early in his career that made a big difference for his business was learning the importance of niche marketing. He says, "It took most of a year of trying to market my own business before I realized that just going out with a shotgun approach wasn't necessarily the best way of doing things."

As soon as he specialized in a niche, in his case Accounting Firms, he got to understand the profession. He learned more about how they operated, who the main firms were and he developed a set of customized marketing materials for his Accountant niche. After that, Richards started to find that his business was getting a little bit easier. "That's how the love affair that I've had for over thirty years with marketing really started," Richards adds.

Richards didn't stay self-employed for his entire career and moved in and out of employment and self-employment several times. For example, he spent time working as a Regional Manager and then State Manager for the largest financial services company in Australia for many years. He was also CEO of the Leukemia Foundation of Australia for a period.

In his second bout of self-employment from 2001, he established a consulting firm Accelerated Outcomes Pty Ltd. He says, "I was older, hopefully a little bit wiser and definitely more experienced." Once again, Richards found that niche marketing was the way forward and began to coach others on how to use niche marketing to grow their own business.

Richards is currently in the process of launching a coaching service with his partner called PetBiz Profits.

"We take people through a three-month coaching program and we implement a five step Authority Marketing process. It's a very comprehensive process that takes pet business owners through positioning as an authority, product creation, being published, promoting through multiple channels and then profiting through multiple revenue streams. For the first round of coaching, we've customized the program for pet store owners, pet retailers, distributors and wholesalers. We also offer a generic version of our program through my main company Accelerated Outcomes for those outside the pet industry and we have plans to expand our offerings for different niche businesses in the future," Richards says.

Though Richards is based in Australia, his business partner is an Englishman who lives in France. Ninety-five percent of the focus of their business, PetBiz Profits, is currently on working with clients in the U.S. who work in the pet industry.

"I've been working with U.S. clients now for about fifteen years," Richards says, "I'm used to the time zone issues and it's definitely possible to run a global coaching and consulting business."

Learn more about Brian Richards and PetBiz Profits at: http://www.PetBizProfits.com or at the Accelerated Outcomes site at http://www.AcceleratedOutcomes.net.

GLEN ROTHQUEL

BUSINESS:	Leads2Profits
WEBSITE:	Leads2profits.net
EMAIL:	info@leads2profits.net
FACEBOOK:	Facebook.com/leads.to.profits
LINKEDIN:	LinkedIn.com/in/glenrothquel
TWITTER:	Twitter.com/leads2profits
LOCATION:	New South Wales, Australia

I've always wanted to work for myself," Glen Rothquel says. "I come from a family of small business owners so I've grown up in that environment and used to love being able to go into the store and help my dad out. I really liked it when I was allowed to help out serving customers and I especially loved it when I could count the takings at the end of the day. My dad worked really hard, but I saw the fruits of his work. We lived well but what I truly admired was how dad was always in control and didn't have a boss telling him what to do or where to go."

Rothquel knew he'd run his own successful business one day — he just didn't know what or when.

"I was working in London in a high pressured, stressful job in investment banking when I decided to do a Cordon Bleu cooking course at one of the top schools in London as a way to relax and learn more, and I absolutely fell in love with the whole environment. There was something relaxing and refreshing about the whole process — going to the markets to buy produce, bringing it back for hours of preparation before cooking the dishes and then happily devouring them with a glass of quality French Bordeaux wine — I was in heaven. Such a contrast to my 'mundane' yet extremely well paid existence in Financial Markets where I regularly made and lost hundreds of thousands of dollars within minutes."

He knew even then that he had to get out and pursue his dream of opening and running a restaurant back in Sydney, Australia. As with many dreams, he let life and family get in the way and never opened the restaurant — something he still regrets to this day. "I did, however, get out of investment banking and go into working for myself," Rothquel explains, "But, I stuck with more "sensible" areas like consulting and finance."

In the past 20 years, Rothquel has bought, sold, started or invested in over 16 businesses in a number of diverse industries from ice cream, to promotional products, to financial advising to solar and many in between. He has had some "spectacular failures" along the way as well as great successes during his career as an entrepreneur. Because of his experience, he now shares this real world knowledge and experiences with other business owners who are willing to be helped.

"I'm one of the proverbial jack of all trades yet master of none," Rothquel explains, "I've not spent 20 years learning and honing one skill to be the consummate professional or specialist. What I bring to the table is an eclectic broad mix of educational theory as I have an MBA combined with, get your hands and knees dirty in the trenches working out how to make payroll...real street smart experience. I'm not a 'this is what the book says' kind of guy. I'm a 'this is what works and doesn't work' kind of guy."

"In London one late night, sitting in the dealing room trying to get out of another massive loss position," Rothquel says, "I decided that enough was enough. There is more to life than money and being wined and dined. And I decided there and then to pack up and move back to Australia...never to be 'employed' again."

Now, Rothquel helps businesses differentiate themselves in a crowded market so they get more qualified leads that convert into customers so they make more profitable sales. First, he builds their authority and expert status in their market through international media and where appropriate, becoming a Best Selling author to position them with a competitive edge.

Next, he sets up automated lead generation and conversion systems and sales funnels. Last, he focuses on helping businesses improve communication with customers and provide exceptional customer service. As a result they spend more money, buy more often, stay with the business longer and regularly refer new prospects to the business which results in more sales, bigger profits and greater business value.

"I can help you grow your business, make bigger profit and have more fun and free time because I've done it many times. I've learned the theory and then I've found out through the school of hard knocks what works and what doesn't, so all I do now is what has been proven to work many times over," Rothquel explains.

"It's the circle of life — instead of being in the kitchen in my dreamed of award-winning restaurant following a proven recipe to make a delicious cake, I now follow a tried, tested and refined recipe to make businesses successful, grow value, and have fun." Says Glen.

"I'm still a closet chef — I love food, wine and cooking, and in my next life, I'm coming back as Jamie Oliver!" Rothquel says. He has a passion for Rugby and loves nothing more than the freedom of snow skiing down challenging black runs at Whistler.

Glen is married to Kath and has two wonderful, independent, successful kids — Nick and Lucy.

KEN SHERMAN

BUSINESS: Go Pro Local

WEBSITE: GoProLocal.com

EMAIL: consult@goprolocal.com

LOCATION: Gilbert, Arizona

FACEBOOK: Facebook.com/ken.sherman2

Ken Sherman, Managing Director of authority marketing agency, Go Pro Local, helps businesses reach their full potential by establishing their online presence; managing their online reputation and helping business owners gain recognition as an authority and expert in their industry. Ken has successfully started and grown several businesses as a serial entrepreneur.

Ken caught the entrepreneurial bug when he was only 5 or 6 years old. His grandparents owned an auto shop in Mountain View, California where Ken would watch the mechanics as they worked. "To see my grandfather in the office, in charge of everything, inspired me to want to be like him someday."

Ken says, "I came from a family where pretty much everyone in my family — my parents, grandparents and even great-grandparents — have all been self-employed. I never felt growing up that I was going to end up working for someone. I always felt like I was going to strike out and do my own thing."

Ken went to college at Arizona State University and got an Aeronautic Engineering degree in 1993, just in time for the whole airline industry to collapse and not have any jobs available when he got out of school. He remembers thinking, 'What am I going to do now?' Soon after that he started a tile and grout cleaning company in Arizona and found success with it quickly.

"I put up a website for my little service business and very quickly I got a phone call from a man in Chicago," Ken explains, "He said, 'I want to come and learn how to do this. I have a handyman business. I'm going to add tile and grout cleaning to my business. How much to teach me?' I said, 'Five grand.' He came out, helped me on my jobs for four days and paid me $5,000. When he left I thought, 'I just made $5,000 off the Internet!' That was it. I was hooked."

Later, Ken expanded his business holdings and bought a company that made one of the products he was using in his restoration business. Ken says, "That's when I realized that this was about more than owning a service business or making money on the Internet, I finally understood that I was an entrepreneur and that I could work on many different businesses and not just one."

About 7 years ago Ken branched out from service industry businesses to help any kind of business from dentists to leather shoe polish companies. "I tend to focus on local businesses — not necessarily local to my market in Arizona— just local small and medium sized businesses as opposed to national chains. I feel like I have a special talent for service businesses because I've owned a service business for so long and helped so many contractors establish an online presence and find new customers," Ken adds.

"I marketed for a client from Texas that started out with no website and then got a website," Ken explains, "Within 10 months; he was making $25,000 a month in business off of his website — for him that was magic."

Ken is an entrepreneur at heart. He has a passion for taking action and overcoming obstacles. Clients find him to be an effective team builder and a great communicator with the ability to take ideas from concept to completion.

"A lot of times, business owners are just stuck in their business — working *in* their business instead of working *on* their business. They can't see the forest for the trees," Ken says, "I'm able to come in and say, 'Look, here's what we can do to generate new business and get your growth kick-started again'. The outside perspective I can bring to business owners is valuable and effective."

Internet Marketing Educator, Jack Mize, always says, "Make more doing less." That hits home for Ken. Ken tells his clients, "Focus in on something that you're good at and stick with that. Work in your talent area and you will see amazing success in your business."

"I had another client in California," Ken adds, "He called me up on a Sunday one time and said, 'Ken, listen, I've got something I've got to talk to you about.' I said, 'What's wrong?' I'm thinking it's weird he's calling on a Sunday. Instead of something wrong, he says, 'Thank you so much...you don't know what you've done for my life. I'm able to put my kids through college. I'm able to pay off a bunch of debt. You've turned everything around for me.' That just inspires me. It's stories like that that just make me love what I do even more. I help businesses open up new channels of revenue by using Internet marketing and websites to generate leads and income and positioning my clients as an educator and advocate for their clients and prospects success...and it makes a real difference in people's lives."

In his down time Ken enjoys spending time with his family, playing piano, learning about technology, motorcycling, racing and most adrenaline inducing activities.

For more information about Ken Sherman visit: https://www.LinkedIn.com/in/kensherman.

Learn more about Go Pro Local at: http://www.goprolocal.com.

LOUIS F. VARGAS

WEBSITE: LocalLeadsHQ.com,
StrategicEdgeProfits.com

EMAIL: Louis@LocalLeadsHQ.com

LOCATION: Las Vegas, NV, Los Angeles, CA

FACEBOOK: Facebook.com/LouisF.Vargas

LinkedIn: LinkedIn.com/in/louisfvargasauthorceo

Twitter: Twitter.com/LouisFVargas

Louis F. Vargas is a mega-successful entrepreneur, author, investor, and a business growth and marketing authority. He is the current founder and CEO of three "Inc. 500" companies: (1) *Local Leads HQ*, a digital media marketing company whose success is its "pay for results-only" model of Pay-Per-Lead (PPL) and Pay-Per-Call (PPC), and a sales training and consulting division, (2) *Strategic Edge Profits*, a business and wealth strategies education firm, and (3) *Universal Media Group, Ltd,* a media publisher of online destination sites for the Hispanic, survivalist, women, entertainment, sports, and hobbyist markets. And he is the former cofounder & CEO of an *Inc. 500* advertising agency that he sold in 2008.

Strategic Edge Profits and Local Leads HQ are a cross between a doctor and an engineer. As doctors we diagnose the sickness a business has --e.g., Why is it about to fail? Why are profits down or stagnant? Where is the market penetration index lagging so much? After we diagnose, we treat the "patient." And as business engineers we design and implement the solutions that allow for fast recovery and growth.

But more than that we are educators and advocates for the success of our clients, no matter what. We just don't simply find and fix problems for our client's businesses, we get vested in their success, we go in, get dirty, stick around until things get turned around and then make sure that EVERYONE in the business (from receptionist to product creation to the Boardroom) is on the same page and same focus for company or business success because they know that the success of the business means more money for raises, better pay, bonuses and job security.

While the executives, CEO and/or business owner or professional knows and understands that our approach will mean more money in the bank! That's why we can charge as much as $10K per day to $29.5K a week for our advice.

Our motto?: "Life Freedom is only possible when you have Financial Freedom." So we help business owners and businesses fix problems that exponentially increase their profits while reducing costs.

Our 5 Main Goals for all clients are:

1. Creating marketing and systems that get you more clients fast.

2. Significantly increase your business profits.

3. Automating all marketing.

4. Creating ROI metrics to make sure the stuff is working.

5. Streamline financial metrics & management Systems.

In his business career he has been responsible for orchestrating campaigns that resulted in sales of over $500 million for companies. He initially started on Wall Street and now consults with businesses and go-getter entrepreneurs on the systems needed to build 7-Figure incomes on auto-pilot, including overlooked sources of internal growth, strategic joint-ventures, guerilla mega-marketing and quick strategic growth using the Authority Mindset blueprint.

He has spoken before the California Legislature and at business conferences, USC, Pepperdine University, and UCLA. He has consulted with small businesses and Fortune 500's and advised companies like AIG Insurance, Ford, Nissan, and GM. He is the author of *The Passion-Driven Life: The Secrets of Success, Balance & Fulfillment in 9 Key Areas of Life* (Morgan-James Pub.: 2010) and the upcoming book *Autopilot 7-Figure Incomes: An Insider Reveals the Strategies, Secrets & Systems Used By The Ultra-Rich to Quickly Build 7-Figure Income Empires on Auto-Pilot.*
"Entrepreneurism has been in my blood before I was even born. My father was an ex-banker who immigrated to America and sought to provide for a large family. During 30

years in business my father started and ran multiple small businesses ranging from construction to bakery to a printing company, among others," Vargas recalls.

True to form as an entrepreneur, some of his ventures were successful while others fizzled. Yet he managed to always move forward in search of another one. "I learned from his tenacity and will to succeed to never give up," Vargas says.

"I caught the entrepreneur bug early on in life and while in high school I worked and saved like all my money, while my peers bought electronics, clothes and frivolously blew their money," he says, "At the age of 16 I started to invest in the stock market."

During graduate school at USC he focused on finding a company or niche where he could hone his investing and marketing skills. Vargas was able to secure a position as an investment broker for a Beverly Hills firm. Once there he learned hands-on real-world things like micro and macro economic cycles, investment ROI, bond swaps & trading, sourcing venture capital, joint ventures, sales, direct marketing and customer service.

"I had many clients who were successful real estate investors and business   owners," Vargas says, "I realized early on that the basis and matrix of wealth begins with ownership of a growing and successful business. So I immersed myself further in finance, marketing, strategic business growth and was mentored by many successful millionaire entrepreneurs who took a liking to my young aggressive zeal to succeed. I took their advice and eventually did."

Besides being hungry to succeed Vargas also had the benefit

of having had many successful multi-millionaire clients from many diverse industries (real estate, manufacturing, professionals, business owners, and CEO's) while he was a young investment adviser. For them, he was able to obtain a collection of wisdom and gems of information on the "what-to-do's" and the "what not-to-do's" regarding success.

He saved his money and was able to make several investments in real estate and the stock market. He also did a few M&A (Mergers and Acquisition) deals for himself. A few years later, he left the investment industry. He started a marketing consulting and a private hedge investment fund to invest in small companies and offer as well business mega-growth and consulting strategies.

The crossing point from being a "I'm going to be an entrepreneur" to an "I am an entrepreneur" was two-fold for Vargas: (1) He was very diligent about educating himself in finance, business, investment and economic cycles, laser focused strategic business growth, out-of-the-box marketing, and effective leadership/management. He was a student of and mentor of world class professors such as management guru Peter Drucker (Claremont), leadership guru Warren Bennis, and supply side economics guru Arthur Laffer (USC).

Moreover he attended many seminars and industry conferences on growth, start-ups, M&A trends, marketing and investing to further enhance his abilities and influencers network, and (2) He purposely sought out and created a master-mind network of influential, wise and successful business people from whom he could ask questions, bounce ideas off, strategize and in some cases create joint-ventures on projects.

With *Local Leads HQ* our mission is to create and implement for our clients new methods of marketing, sizzling and mega-successful direct marketing campaigns without breaking the bank, and install new client acquisition and retention strategies and systems geared to getting a massive amount of prospects/leads month after month. Also we create effective and measurable internal sales conversion funnels and systems where our clients can maintain a constant connection with existing clients and prospects, revive old clients, and increase the amount and frequency of business transaction from clients.

Strategic Edge Profits is what I am most passionate about. It allows middle income earners, entrepreneurs, and "wanna-be entrepreneurs" to obtain access to a world-class real-world "brain-trust" of successful millionaire, multi-millionaire and even billionaire entrepreneurs and business owners, get actionable financial and wealth education, and work on fast wealth acquisition strategies. We have a members-only model where we build relationships, mentor, connect with others, provide resources, invest in deals [a smaller scale "Shark Tank"], create finance channels, and help others "build a better mousetrap", make money and encourage charity.

Our mission is to empower entrepreneurs, Main Street business owners and middle class income earners to explore, understand and implement the not-so-well-known insider strategies, systems, and secrets used and known (and reserved until now) mainly for and by the ultra-rich to create current high passive income and build 6 to 7-figure retirement income streams on auto-pilot. *We want our members to have life freedom that is only capable when financial freedom exists.*

At both *Local Leads HQ and Strategic Edge Profits* we have the expertise, experience, connections, technology and systems to dramatically increase our clients income by massively increasing their new client-customer base, and by educating them on the investments, strategies, advice, and resources previously reserved only for the ultra-wealthy.

Vargas enjoys teaching people and advising business owners on how to create and achieve a 7-figure empires on auto-pilot. He also teaches his clients how to achieve financial freedom while balancing their personal lives. He loves traveling, art, reading, museums, sports, spending time with his family, volunteering, charity work, photography, speaking and immersing himself in new strategies for business, investing, finance, and personal and business growth.

To learn more about Louis F. Vargas visit his LinkedIn profile at
http://www.LinkedIn.com/in/louisfvargasauthorceo

Information about his companies, *Local Leads HQ, Strategic Edge Profits* and *Universal Media Group, Ltd.,* can be found online at: LocalLeadsHQ.com, StrategicEdgeProfits.com, and UniMediaLtd.com.